For the Inner Spirit
without Whom this would not have been possible

Contents

Preface

This book is based on the principles and philosophy of *A Course in Miracles*, which will be referred to here as the Course. If you have not read or studied or even heard of the Course, everything you need to learn a new way of forgiveness can be found in this book. The philosophy, the techniques, the mental exercises, all are presented in a complete way.

If you are familiar with the Course and have read through some of the Text and perhaps done the Workbook lessons, this book takes all of that knowledge and shows how by focusing on a simple, straightforward method of forgiveness, the promise of the Course can be yours. For those who have read other books about the Course, we will take a slightly different approach in this book, and some of that difference will relate to the language we use.

Much of the terminology of the Course is Christian in origin, but these Christian terms, like Son of God or Holy Spirit, mean something different from what they mean in the Christian Church. In addition, for those who are not from a Christian background, these terms may be off-putting and may lead to people rejecting the Course before they fully understand what is being said.

The fundamental philosophy of the Course is not Christian or Muslim or Buddhist or like any other religion. At the same time it is fundamentally not anti-Christian or anti- any other religion. There is only one fundamental belief required to understand the Course, and that is the existence of God, though the God described in the Course may be different from what you are used to.

But even if you do not believe in God, if you are only in a very small way open to the possibility of God's existence, there is something to be found in this book. That small openness or willingness is all that's required to see the amazing possibilities of this philosophy. What we will try to do here is show you how your everyday experience is ultimately the result of the existence of this God, and the freedom we have to create our own experience.

In this book, other than using the word God, we will generally not use the Christian terms in the way the Course uses them. From this point forward, the only use of Christian words and phrases will be in regard to the sections on how forgiveness is expressed in different cultures and religions. For example, in place of the term Holy Spirit, we will use Inner Spirit, with the understanding you can replace this with any other term you like which conveys the meaning for you.

The whole point is to present the principles and philosophy to the broadest audience possible without alienating anyone by the use of uncomfortable language. Ultimately we will see in this philosophy that language does not really matter at all, but our hope is this approach will make the concepts more approachable, and ultimately, more meaningful and potentially life-changing.

Introduction

The idea of forgiveness is central to almost every religion in the world, and is a core principle in much of modern psychology. It is also fundamental to the philosophy of the Course. This universality makes forgiveness a common approach to releasing feelings of resentment and anger, and is therefore important to everyone seeking a better way of life.

In this book, we will learn how forgiveness fits into the ancient and modern belief systems, and how forgiveness is expressed differently in all these philosophies. Everyone has an internal picture of what an act of forgiveness should look like, but this picture is strongly influenced by one's own beliefs about religion or psychology, and it will vary widely from one person to the next.

The importance of forgiveness varies among the different religions. In the Christian tradition, it holds a central role as a way for one to eliminate resentment in order to be free to love one's neighbor. In other Western traditions, forgiveness is emphasized much less. In some traditions, a person is not expected to forgive unless the guilty party has first asked for forgiveness. In others, the forgiveness can be independent of the other person's choices.

There is also a belief within the Western religions that we are all sinners in some form or another, which means we need to ask God's forgiveness for our sins. This goes with the idea we are guilty and therefore in order to receive forgiveness from God, we must first repent for our sins and ask for this forgiveness. This assumes God is ultimately a judgmental God that only grants forgiveness when appropriate.

In Hinduism, we find similar concepts of forgiveness and indeed there are two different methods, one where there is an expectation of the guilty party repenting first, and another where forgiveness is given unconditionally. In Buddhism, forgiveness is a process through which one can realize the delusional nature of the acts that caused pain and of the feelings of anger and resentment these engendered. This is more similar to the form of forgiveness which will be presented in this book.

In the early days of modern psychology, forgiveness was barely considered, but today it is a core technique in many therapies. Studies have been done comparing the mental health of those who forgive and those who do not. In all of these different therapies, it is assumed that forgiving another will release negative emotions and lead to a happier, healthier life.

No matter what the tradition, forgiveness is always difficult. It seems as if our natural tendency is to hold onto resentments and anger and to see our friends and enemies and neighbors as all guilty at some time or another. In order to forgive, we have to give up something that defines who we are, the powerful emotions of anger and even hate. We are told to love everyone by our religious leaders, but we see these leaders express anger at times, so finding examples of purely loving individuals seems almost impossible.

Our plan in this book is to discover a new way of looking at forgiveness, one which does not require contrition from a guilty party, one which does not require any external act on our parts, and one which occurs solely within the mind. This process of forgiveness has the potential to free us from all of our negative thoughts and to open our minds to a true experience of love. With this practice, you have for the first time in your life, the possibility of becoming a purely loving and kind person.

In order to understand how this forgiveness works, we will first outline the philosophy that underpins it. In this philosophy we will discover a concept of God which differs from that of any of the major religions, a God of Pure Mind and Pure Love. By understanding this God, we will discover where we have taken a wrong turn and how truly simple it is to return to the experience of God. However, simple does not mean easy, because we must overcome our resistance to Love in order to find our way Home. We will discover how we have come to accept the idea of separation and how it has fundamentally cut us off from the experience of love in our lives.

Our process of forgiveness is about freeing ourselves from separation in all its forms. When we do, all that will be left is the Loving Mind of God, our True Home. Through practicing forgiveness, we can begin the journey out of the world of pain and anger and guilt, and along that journey we will discover how beautiful and loving our experience of the world can become. For the world will be transformed as we transform our minds. It always starts with the mind and if we heal the mind, the experience of love will be revealed.

It's important to understand that this philosophy and this brand of forgiveness go hand in hand. You can't have one without the other. If you don't accept the fundamentals of the philosophy, this way of forgiveness will not work. This does not mean you have to have a complete, committed belief in the philosophy, but it does mean you need to have an open mind. You need to be willing to allow for the possibility it may be true. Such a willingness will allow you to build your belief as you practice the process of forgiveness that is outlined here. Once you see the changes occurring in your life, practicing forgiveness will reinforce your belief in the philosophy.

On the other hand, if you read and understand and grow to accept the philosophy, but don't develop a regular practice of forgiveness, no real change can happen in your life. It is through this practice you can begin to see the world in a new way. If you only think about, discuss, cogitate on the philosophy without doing the practical work of forgiving, this will just be an intellectual exercise. This book is not about the intellect; it is about finding our way Home, and realizing through forgiveness that everything we thought about the world is illusory. Practicing forgiveness is the path to that realization.

This book is above all a practical book. In the beginning we will look at how forgiveness is taught in the different religions around the world and in modern psychology. We will then present a synopsis of the philosophy which will provide the foundation for learning forgiveness. For the rest of the book we will learn through simple steps and extensive examples, how to practice forgiveness. All you need to bring to this learning are the thoughts within your mind. We will use these thoughts and apply forgiveness and show you the immediate changes that can take place.

If you follow the practice we teach you and apply this practice in your everyday life, you will become a very different person, a person who sees kindness and love in the world, who knows where our True Home lies, and who has accepted that the path back to God is one we can truly follow. This book has the potential to change everything in your life without changing the circumstances of your life. For all the change will occur within your mind and within your perception, and this is the most profound change you will ever experience.

Many Ways to Forgive

Forgiveness is a universal idea. Almost every religion and belief system in the world considers it to be at least one of the tools one can use to live a better life. However, the importance of forgiveness within a particular system of thought or religion varies greatly, as is the way it is applied in different situations. Though everyone knows the word, the meaning is highly dependent on one's experience and upbringing.

In this book we are going to present a particular method of forgiveness based on a fundamental philosophy. This method is applicable to any circumstance in which you find yourself, and once learned, can lead to real change. But before we learn this way of forgiveness, it is important we understand how the rest of the world views forgiveness, and it is important to see how an idea as simple as this can be expressed so differently in different cultures.

Each of you comes to this book with a particular idea of what forgiveness is and how it should be applied. That idea is the sum of all of your experience in life, whether through religion, psychology, or simply through interacting with others. We hope in this chapter you may recognize your particular view of forgiveness, and at the same time learn how other cultures view this idea. You should come away from this with a deeper understanding of all the ways of forgiveness. Once we have this as a basis, we will proceed to our philosophy and learn a very specific way to forgive which you can use in every situation in your life.

The exploration in this chapter will necessarily be a broad overview of these religious and philosophical traditions rather than an in-depth study. Our purpose is not to gain a deep understanding of these traditions, but to see how each specifically addresses the concept of forgiveness. We will begin with the three main Western religions – Judaism, Christianity, and Islam, followed by the Eastern religions – Hinduism, Buddhism, Confucianism, and Taoism. We will look at how the great philosophers have approached forgiveness, and finally we will examine forgiveness as practiced in modern psychology.

Judaism

The Jewish religion is one of the oldest continuously observed beliefs in the world. Though the dates are not known for sure, Abraham's life is often considered a starting point and he lived four thousand or more years ago. Judaism is the foundation for all Western religions, and many of the basic tenets are carried into the Christian and Muslim faiths, including forgiveness. However we will see in the next sections that the nature of forgiveness is actually quite different in each of these Western faiths.

Judaic tradition is centered in the Law. A devout Jew tries to observe the Law, and when one fails, a sin is committed. The person is judged guilty by the Jewish religious society (and ultimately by God) for having broken the Law. The Law that is followed comes from the Hebrew scriptures and is considered to be a given to a devout Jew. There is no need for faith or any kind of external proof, only for observance of the Law. Ultimately it is assumed this Law comes from God, and violations of the Law are acts against God.

There is an assumption in Judaism that each of us has an internal sense of moral right and wrong, but it is not always clear – therefore the need for Jewish Laws to help guide us in our actions. Once these Laws have been learned, one will know when a violation has occurred and will take appropriate actions to atone for the guilt. As in most secular laws, it is not an excuse you did not understand the Law. Through education in the Hebrew scriptures, every Jew should know the right way to act.

When one commits a sin against another person, whether it be an act of anger, theft, physical attack, or any other violation of Jewish law, it is expected the transgressor should seek forgiveness from the one who was wronged. This forgiveness must be earned, it must be deserved, it must be requested and, above all, it can be granted only by the offended person. The process of seeking out the person wronged and apologizing and asking for forgiveness is fundamental to the process in Judaism.

If the wronged party refuses to forgive the transgressor, even after being asked for forgiveness, then the wronged one is considered to have committed a sin, and the transgressor needs to do nothing further. The corollary to this is that one never needs to forgive another person who has harmed oneself unless the other person asks for forgiveness. Therefore forgiveness for acts between individuals is always a two-way process.

It is also assumed that throughout one's life, one will violate God's laws at times, and therefore will need to seek forgiveness from God. Again there is a clear distinction here. If one sins against another person, he asks for forgiveness from that person. If one sins against God, he asks God for forgiveness. This means one needs to understand the Jewish Law adequately so he can determine when and where to ask for this forgiveness.

Yom Kippur is the Day of Atonement in the Jewish tradition. On the eve of this day, it is expected that a devout Jew should take care of forgiving anything which hasn't been forgiven in the last year, and to seek forgiveness for any of his acts which are left unforgiven. Then on Yom Kippur one asks God's forgiveness for any sins one has committed against God.

There is debate around the question of whether some sins, such as rape and murder, are unforgivable. If one commits murder, obviously he cannot ask forgiveness from the person he murdered, at least not in this life. There are also some sins against

God, such as taking idols over God or believing in multiple gods, which may be considered unforgivable by God.

Christianity

Christianity begins with the life of Jesus of Nazareth around two thousand years ago. Jesus was considered a prophet, and his life was seen as holy through a number of miraculous events and through his teachings. Jesus said he was the Christ, the Son of God, and following his death and resurrection, his disciples codified his teachings, which became the New Testament of the Bible. The Old Testament is a rewriting of the older Jewish texts.

The Christian church grew in the early centuries after Jesus' death, and in a few hundred years split into the Western Roman Catholic and the Eastern Orthodox sects. In the 16th century, Martin Luther started the Protestant reformation and today the Christian church consists of over 500 different sects spread around the world, becoming the largest religion in the world.

Jesus' message was one of love and kindness and forgiveness, though according to the accounts of his life, he did not always act in this manner. However, in these accounts, he is said to have healed the sick and infirm, to have fed the multitudes with only a few loaves and fishes, and even to have raised the dead. He had many enemies who either did not believe him, or did not want to see the old religious order upset by his teachings. This ultimately led to his crucifixion, and then to his resurrection, according to the accounts.

In spite of his message of love, there is a strong element of judgment and fear in the religion. If one does not in some way repent for one's sins, God will be the ultimate judge, with the idea of some kind of punishment in the offing. There is a sense one should be loving and kind out of fear, not because it is the natural way to act. In fact in much of the subsequent Christian writing, humans are portrayed as fundamentally flawed and only through great effort can we come close to freeing ourselves from sin.

Forgiveness is considered a central theme in Christianity. Jesus refers often to forgiving one another and also to praying to God for forgiveness. In Christianity, we do not see the same differentiation between sins against another person and sins against God which is taught in Judaism. One can ask, through prayer, for God to forgive one's transgression against another person. In some sects, this might require some act of repentance, but it does not necessarily require asking for forgiveness from the other party.

It is, however, always considered important for us to forgive others for what we perceive to be transgressions against us. Holding on to resentment means we are not able to fully express love to the people in our lives. To the extent we are not expressing love, we are then also committing a sin. Therefore forgiveness is of great importance in trying to lead a sinless life. It is essential to realize in this religion that all these acts against us and the ones we commit are considered very real and must be addressed in order to gain God's love and forgiveness.

From a Judaic point of view, this might seem to be a bit too easy. We can commit as many sins as we like, and at any point, even on our deathbed, if we ask God for forgiveness and accept Christ as our Savior, all is forgiven. Where is the justice in all this? The reality is if you believe in the Christian teachings, even though there is an element of judgment, there is less of a sense of justice and retribution, and more of a sense of loving everyone, no matter what the behavior.

In the New Testament, the only sin which is mentioned as being unforgivable is 'blasphemy against the Holy Spirit.' This has been interpreted a number of ways, but fundamentally it means if you do not accept and worship God, then you will not be forgiven when the moment of judgment comes. In essence, it is saying if you are not a Christian, you will not be forgiven for your sins. All other sins, as far as the teachings say, can be forgiven by repenting and asking for God's forgiveness.

Islam

The religion of Islam began in the 7th century through the teachings of the prophet Muhammad. The holy book, called the Qur'an, is believed by Muslims to be the literal word of God, or Allah, and was revealed to Muhammad. They believe there were previous prophets, including Moses, Abraham, and Jesus, but the teachings from these prophets had become distorted, and the Qur'an is God's final revelation. The Qur'an in Arabic is considered the only word of God, and all other translations are only interpretations.

In Islam, God is the ultimate end. Pre-Islamic society was not one of evil, but one of ignorance and ingratitude. Islam means submission to God, a submission which is total and irrevocable for a devout Muslim. There are five pillars, or essential acts, in the Islamic faith. These are the creed ("I testify there are no deities other than God alone and I testify that Muhammad is the Messenger of God."), the five daily ritual prayers, fasting from dawn to dusk during Ramadan, alms-giving or helping the poor and needy, and a pilgrimage to Mecca at least once in one's lifetime.

In the Qur'an, divine forgiveness is key. It is an essential attribute of God and of the Prophet, and is to be emulated by all followers of the faith. It begins with a recognition of the transgression, whether this is realized by the individual or shown by an external authority. Then one must have a change of heart and ask for God's forgiveness, as well as providing compensation to anyone harmed by the act. There is a complete acceptance that the injured party was truly injured and both parties must deal with the injury. Practically Muslims are not unlike others in feeling guilty about acts they have committed and seeking resolution and redemption for this guilt.

Islam treats true believers differently from those who do not believe in Islam or those who are considered infidels or blasphemous. This has led outsiders to sometimes view Islam suspiciously. In regard to forgiveness, one's behavior is different toward believers and non-believers. One should forgive another believer, knowing there will be understanding of how and why the forgiveness is given. For non-believers, retribution is acceptable and it is expected God will judge and punish them as well. As with most of the Western religions, there is separation between those who are part of the faith and those who are not. In Islam this separation is more pronounced.

The Qur'an is a guide for individuals to help them morally choose right from wrong. When a person becomes aware of his own guilt, the emphasis is not to dwell on guilt, but to release it through repentance and returning to God. Sin in Islam is willfully acting in opposition to God's will, and is considered to be more a weakness than something evil. What actions are sinful are spelled out in the Qur'an, and there is always the possibility of asking for God's forgiveness for one's sins. Each person can go to God alone, since there is no need for any priestly intervention.

Muslims believe in free will, and like in Judaism and Christianity, this means constantly making moral choices in life, choices which affect one's relationship to God. It is understood one will on occasion disobey God, but mercy and forgiveness can always be requested. The one thing God will not forgive is ingratitude for all the mercies God has given. The submission to God means one must accept God totally and turn to God for all matters, including forgiveness.

Hinduism

Hinduism is one of the oldest religions in the world, and through the ages, it has evolved into different sects and traditions. Modern Hindus observe many different forms of Hinduism; devotion to multiple deities, yogic practices, focus on good works, meditation, and a variety of other forms.

There are many ancient writings, the Vedas, which represent the foundation of Hindu belief. After the Vedas, came a host of other writings, including the Upanishads, and perhaps the most important work in modern Hinduism, the Bhagavad-Gita. This was written around the time of Jesus' life, and consists of a series of dialogs between the warrior Arjuna and the god Krishna. These dialogs represent a concise presentation of the Hindu philosophy.

Two important concepts in Hinduism are karma and dharma. Hindus believe in reincarnation, the cycle of death and rebirth. Karma represents a natural process of cause and effect, wherein one can, through right actions, eventually be free of this cycle. Conversely through wrong moral actions one may descend the ladder of rebirth to a lower standing in the next life. The moral traditions of Western religions are focused on the impact an individual's actions have on another. In Hinduism and Buddhism, a person follows a moral path in order to better oneself.

Dharma is conformity to a moral duty that is inherent in all living things. It includes the rituals one must undertake in life, as well as one's vocation and one's relationships with others. It represents all that is right and good in the universe, and living in accordance with dharma brings one closer to personal liberation.

Forgiveness is mentioned a number of times in the Bhagavad-Gita, but it is not as central to the religion as it is in Western religions. It is considered part of the process of living a good life, one of kindness, compassion, and helpfulness to others. Though there are some references to seeking forgiveness from a god in certain writings, this again is not a major theme. Forgiveness seems to be more something one does as part of leading a moral life. Clearly if one withholds forgiveness, one will retain anger and resentment, which will impact one's karma.

In some of these references, there is the concept of a feminine form of forgiveness, associated with the god Lakshmi, and a masculine form, associated with the god Vishnu. In the feminine form, which is more like Christianity, one should forgive another no matter whether the other person repents or not. In the masculine form, similar to Judaism, there is no requirement to forgive unless the other person repents first. The feminine form is considered a higher form, leading to a greater easing of one's karma.

As in other religions, there is often discussion of whether some acts, such as rape or murder, are truly unforgivable. Since there is a huge volume of writings over many centuries in the Hindu tradition, opinion varies and there is no clear consensus. Based on the law of karma, the one committing a grievous act, will surely impact his karma whether he is forgiven or not. Washing away of such seemingly sinful acts through asking a higher power for forgiveness may or may not be effective based on which writings one follows.

There is a point where one can, through meditation and good works, reach a highly self-realized state, a state where one is living a life of goodness and peace and forgiveness every minute of the day. At this point, the world is seen in a different light, and one's actions can carry one beyond the law of karma to true oneness with all things.

Buddhism

Siddhartha Gautama (later known as the Buddha) lived sometime between the 6th and 5th centuries BC. He grew up in a life of privilege, but after attaining adulthood, he observed suffering in the world and decided to dedicate his life to understanding this suffering and finding a path to liberation. He went on a spiritual quest trying a variety of different practices and concluded the right path was the Middle Way, which came somewhere between everyday life and the life of the extreme ascetic.

This path included regular meditation and compassion for all life. He famously achieved enlightenment while meditating under a sacred fig tree, the Bodhi tree. He eventually started a monastic order and it was through his oral teachings that we learn of his philosophy. The first writings of Buddhism did not appear until two centuries after the Buddha died, and therefore there are no divinely inspired writings in Buddhism.

In Buddhism there is no God as Westerners think of God. Instead there is the state of Nirvana, a state of emptiness where all dualities disappear. It is a state which is impossible to describe in words and must be experienced through meditation. Consequently there is no God to please or displease and no God to judge a person's behavior or to grant forgiveness.

Buddha teaches the four Noble Truths – the existence of suffering, how suffering is caused by attachment, how suffering ends when we liberate attachments, and the path to achieving that liberation. The path is referred to as the Eightfold Path – right views, right intent, right speech, right conduct, right livelihood, right effort, mindfulness, and concentration.

Karma exists in Buddhism in a way similar to Hinduism. Through following the path to liberation, one can end the cycle of death and rebirth. This is achieved both through inner meditation and right action in the world. When we feel anger or hatred toward another, this can have a negative effect on our karma. Conversely, when we act in a kind and compassionate way toward others, there is a positive effect upon karma.

Therefore, it is to our benefit to deal with feelings of anger, hatred, and resentment, and this can be achieved through a kind of forgiveness. In Buddhism, since there is no God personality we can go to for forgiveness, we must find a way to forgive on our own. This is achieved through meditation and through examining the deep underlying cause of the negative feelings, which is our attachment to suffering. This attachment and this suffering is ultimately an illusion. The focus here is on changing our thoughts and not on performing any specific deeds to achieve forgiveness. Forgiveness happens within.

As one follows the Eightfold Path, it is expected that resentments and hatreds will fade away. Through a loving kindness toward the world, through meditation to touch the deeper parts of ourselves, and through understanding how the mind works, we can lead a life free of negative thoughts and experiences. As we are learning, though, there will be times when we need to forgive others and to forgive ourselves for our lack of understanding.

Forgiveness is not a core element of Buddhism, but it is a useful tool as one attempts to work through one's karma and seek enlightenment through meditation. The fundamental core of Buddhist action is compassion and loving kindness and this is the emphasis in Buddhist teaching. Unlike the Western religions, forgiveness is not necessary, but can be helpful.

Confucianism & Taoism

There has been debate for centuries about how to classify Confucianism. Since there is no deity and no description of a world beyond this one, it is difficult to call it a religion. It is an ethical philosophy, but one which has permeated the Chinese society in such a way, it is hard to distinguish between the teachings of Confucius and ordinary societal norms. As a philosophy, it is closest to the Western ideas of humanism.

Confucius (or Kongfuzi) was born in 551 BC and lived into his 70's. As an adult he originally pursued a government career, but was only mildly successful. Eventually he started a school to train young men for public service, and it was from these teachings his philosophy developed. He left only very brief writings, but one hundred years later, one of his disciples, Mencius (or Meng Zi), wrote a book of sayings, called the Book of Mencius, which has become the core text of Confucianism.

The concept of virtue is central to Confucianism. One should lead a life of positive moral duty, a life of warm-hearted expression, charity, and compassion toward one's fellow man. This sense of duty starts toward one's family, and extends to the community, including not only the immediate community where one lives, but also the wider community of the world. One is expected to be honest in all dealings with others, and to always speak the truth. Confucianism even includes a Golden Rule – Do not do to others what you do not want them to do to you.

Taoism (or Daoism) is based on the teachings of Lao Tzu (or Laozi), who may have lived around the fourth century BC, and other later teachers, and is a much more mystical tradition than Confucianism. The book, the Tao Te Ching (or Dao De Jing), contains teachings attributed to Lao Tzu. This philosophy is based on the way of the Tao, the underlying source and energy of all things. In a way similar to Zen Buddhism, one can never truly speak of the Tao, but can only experience it. Out of these experiences, the teachings include more practical aspects of living a life in accordance with the principle of the Tao.

Among these are the three treasures, which are usually translated as compassion, moderation, and humility. One who follows the Tao sees the goodness in life and strives to live according to these principles. One does not exert their will against the natural order of things, but lives a life of 'effortless action', or sometimes, 'non-action'. This requires getting in touch with the natural order through concentration or meditation, and once connected to this path, acting in a way that follows this basic order.

In regard to forgiveness, we find Confucianism, which is more focused on societal action, allows for retribution and justice in certain instances. In others, it is understood forgiveness will lead to greater harmony in society. It is up to a follower to understand how to apply forgiveness in any particular situation. The choice to forgive is much more a practical, ethical decision than it is a religious one. There is no God who is watching what you decide.

In Taoism, we find a situation much closer to Buddhism, where the focus is on merging our will with the Tao, and acting in a kind, compassionate, humble way in the world. Though forgiveness is not focused on specifically, part of acting in a compassionate, humble way is to forgive those who appear to have acted against you. This would also include apologizing and seeking forgiveness for acts which you have mistakenly inflicted upon another. It all comes down to finding the peaceful, Tao way of acting in the world.

The Philosophers

We will now examine forgiveness in the context of the philosophy of reason, the tradition which began in ancient Greece and gained momentum with the Renaissance and a new scientific, materialist view of the world. In a way similar to Confucianism, these philosophies seek to find a path to leading a moral, happy life without the absoluteness of God and religion.

The ancient Greek schools of philosophy begin with the writings of the two most famous philosophers, Plato and Aristotle. These writings influenced non-religious philosophy for over two thousand years. The basis of the philosophy is virtue and the ultimate good is happiness, not just simple bodily pleasure, but a full intellectual and emotional happiness derived from the pursuit of excellence.

The rewards of leading this virtuous life were for the here and now, not for a relationship with God or for an afterlife. By pursuing this life of virtue, one seeks to live a life of honor, courage, and nobility of character. One avoids extremes and tries to find a middle path, using our basic goodness and conscience as a guide. This basic goodness is a core principle which runs counter to some other philosophies and religions.

Following the fall of Greek culture and later the Roman Empire, the Middle Ages were a time dominated by religious thought, and the philosophy of reason took a backseat in the Western world. With the dawn of the Renaissance in the 1400's, reason, and especially the ideas of science came to the forefront. For the next four hundred years, philosophical thought began to compete head-on with religious thought, something unthinkable in the Middle Ages.

Many schools of philosophy were developed during this time and many philosophers became widely known, much more so than today. Of the different schools, some were complete opposites of each other and there was a great volume of writings as one school would defend their ideas against another. Among the more famous were Newton, Leibniz, Descartes, Berkeley, Hobbes, Mill, Kant, and Nietzsche.

In Aristotle's original writings, forgiveness was not considered a virtue. In this and the later schools of thought which focus on virtue and moral duty, there is no presumption one must forgive. Instead there is an acceptance there will always be situations where retribution is the appropriate response. Forgiveness is nice in certain situations, because it is a good thing to do, but when the other party shows no signs of remorse, or the other party threatens one repeatedly, forgiveness is not encouraged.

In fact in some philosophies, notably that of Nietzsche, forgiveness may be seen as a sign of weakness. As we are trying to exhibit courage, nobility, and ultimately a form of personal power, forgiving someone might encourage the transgressor to attack us again. We do not need to strike back in anger, but we do need to stand our ground so we will not be easily defeated. Seeking forgiveness from another would equally be a sign of weakness, since internal guilt is considered a great failing.

This gives us an indication of where human thought will go when there is no higher moral authority than one's own mind and conscience. Without a deity to provide us with a roadmap for our lives, we can only use reason and logic to decide how to act, and if one thinks reasonably, defending oneself against an attack would seem the most appropriate response. We can forgive if somehow we are contributing to our own well-being or to a greater good, but there is no imperative for us to forgive in all instances of attack.

Modern Psychology

From ancient times to the early 19th century, the study of the mind was considered to be the purview of philosophy. Philosophers address questions of thought, emotion, morality, and how we as humans make decisions, all aspects of the mind. The term 'psychology' was first used in the 16th century, but was not widely used until the late 18th century. Often the term 'mental philosophy' was used, but beginning in the late 19th century psychology became the accepted term, and an attempt was made to use more scientific principles in this study. This was the beginning of psychology as a discipline separate from philosophy.

Throughout Europe and America, a new field of experimental psychology evolved. Tests were devised to measure the performance and reactions of different individuals when given a particular task or stimulus. By measuring these responses across a large number of people, statistical averages of behavior could be determined, and hypotheses of the behavior of the mind could be formed and tested.

Some of these psychologists wanted to measure only the exterior behavior of these individuals and others wanted to understand the thinking processes which led to a particular response. This ultimately created a split among the experimental psychologists which persists to the modern day. Those focusing on only external behavior formed the field of behaviorism, and those considering the internal mental processes formed the field of cognitive psychology. Other branches and sub-branches of psychology have come and gone over the last century.

In the late 19th century, Sigmund Freud began a practice of psychiatry and over the next twenty years he would formulate, primarily through observations of his own case studies, his theories of psychoanalysis. His ideas were very influential through the first half of the 20th century and still have adherents today. These theories focused mainly on the unconscious mind and repressed sexual memories and fantasies from childhood. He developed the method of talk therapy to try to get the patient to bring these unconscious thoughts to the surface.

Freud and the other psychological researchers from the late 19th and early 20th centuries paid very little attention to the idea of forgiveness. Their focus was on understanding behavior and the unconscious mind. In the last forty years or so, there has been an increasing awareness of forgiveness as a therapeutic tool, which has led to a great deal of research into forgiveness, including many double-blind studies looking at how forgiveness can heal relationships and lead to a better quality of life.

In the psychological realm, forgiveness is a process of letting go of resentment and anger toward an offender. While acknowledging feelings of anger, one can begin to look beyond the anger and see a past transgression in a kinder, more peaceful way. It is essentially a personal process whereby we release our own anger and resentment in spite of what happened to us.

This process does not mean one should forget what happened, nor excuse or condone the action. In the therapeutic context, part of the process of forgiveness is to fully experience the pain of the action against you, knowing it was very real and hurtful. It is important to admit and embrace one's suffering in order to move beyond it. Only then can one let go of these feelings and see the whole experience in a new light.

As you forgive another, there can be no real expectation the other party will understand what was done to you, or what your feelings are about the act. The one who is a transgressor in your eyes may not realize they did anything bad at all and therefore may never admit to any wrong-doing. Forgiveness is fundamentally a process for self-healing and if the other party is open to exploring forgiveness with you, then it can in some cases be helpful in healing relationships as well.

Research has shown that when forgiveness is applied properly, participants see a variety of positive effects. They seem happier with life, healthier due to reduced stress, better able to relate to those close to them without fear, and feel kinder and more connected to everyone they come in contact with. These positive benefits have led some counselors to become full-time forgiveness therapists, using forgiveness as the core process for healing.

One important element in this therapeutic process is to learn to heal oneself. All of us have feelings of guilt related to past actions we have taken, which we believe have hurt someone. In the process of learning to forgive others, one also has to look at one's anger and resentment toward oneself, and learn to release it. This can lead to a greater sense of well-being and self-love and self-confidence, which can help in how we relate to others.

Of course, because some people want to hang onto resentment and anger, the process of forgiveness is not universally successful. As with any therapy, forgiveness will work only for some patients. Other therapies may be more successful for these individuals, so for the vast majority of therapists, forgiveness is just considered one tool in an arsenal of techniques for mental healing.

Some Common Themes

Now that we have looked at all the different ways people throughout the world view forgiveness, it is useful to look at some of the commonality among all these perspectives on forgiveness. With the possible exception of some of the more mystical sects of Hinduism and Buddhism, throughout all of these disparate systems of thought, we find several common themes and assumptions. These include,

- We as humans are real physical beings inhabiting a real physical world within a real physical universe.

- This is true no matter what story we believe about why we are here, or whether we believe there is a life beyond this world. While we are here we are experiencing a real world.

- As humans we will on occasion become angry and resentful toward another person. The process of forgiveness we believe in is a way to release our anger and resentment.

- On occasion we will hurt another human, whether psychologically, emotionally, or physically. In any case, the hurt we inflict is real. You can help release your guilt by seeking forgiveness for yourself.

- If we believe in a God, and if we believe we have violated one of God's laws, we can ask God for forgiveness. This process may require specific acts of repentance.

- If we do not believe in God, then there are no external laws to violate and our actions will be based on some other internal rules and beliefs.

- In all of these instances, what we are forgiving or what we are asking forgiveness for is something real and actual and potentially lasting.

In the next chapter we are going to examine the philosophy which will be the foundation for the method of forgiveness you will learn in this book. We will discover how this fundamental philosophy describes a very different world from the one which is so familiar to us, but we will also discover how this new way of looking at the world has the potential to free us from all the pain, fear, anger, and guilt we experience in our lives. This way of forgiving holds the promise to make us more loving, compassionate, and peaceful.

The Philosophy

Having explored how forgiveness is viewed by many of the people in the world, we are now ready to explore our philosophy and see how this way of forgiveness can change our lives. As mentioned earlier, this philosophy is based on the principles of *A Course in Miracles*. If you have never heard of the Course or have only briefly explored it, it doesn't matter. Everything you need to learn this philosophy and this way of forgiveness is presented here.

Everyone who reads this book will come to it with some preconceived notions about God and the nature of this world we live in. For many of you, the ideas presented here may seem strange and may contradict what you currently believe about the world. The picture of God may be very different than anything you have been taught. The method of forgiveness may not conform to any of the ideas you have read before. Your first reaction to some of these ideas may be resistance and even resentment.

All that is being asked of you is that you keep an open mind as you read, and you stick with it until you have had a chance to see the incredible potential this way of seeing the world will offer you. There is something wonderful in these ideas – the possibility of dramatically changing your life from one of pain and fear and guilt to one of love. If you keep this goal in mind and at least temporarily turn off your critical thinking, you will be much more likely to let these ideas into your mind.

You are not being asked to accept these ideas because they sound good or because some authority has given them to you. You are being asked to simply listen to what this philosophy is about and to learn the fundamental practice of forgiveness for yourself, regardless of where the ideas come from. Once you have begun a regular practice, and only then, will you be able to judge whether this process works. It is hoped if you do follow through and implement the practice, the fundamental change in your life for the better will encourage you to continue, and the source of the ideas will no longer matter to you.

The philosophy begins with some assumptions about the nature of God and the Natural State of Being. In this philosophy, the existence of God is unquestioned, though this God varies significantly from the God of most religions. Most importantly, this God is Mind and only Mind, and anything we believe that exists, other than Mind, is simply an illusion.

We will see how the idea of separation is a core concept, and how our belief in separation has led us to believe we exist within a world external to ourselves. We will then learn how through forgiveness we can free ourselves of this illusion of separation and how we can move beyond the negative experience of our lives to re-experience our Natural State of Peace within a Loving God.

God

This God is a God of Oneness, unlimited by time and space. The world we believe we live in is a world of duality, seemingly bound by time and space. Though it is possible to have direct experience of our Oneness with God while still living in this world, this requires we must temporarily step outside this world. And because ours is a world of duality, we can never fully describe the experience of Oneness while we believe we occupy this world.

However, in order to understand the experience of our everyday world, in this philosophy we need to talk about God from a dualistic point of view at times – describing what God is like and what God is not like. Our goal is to get as close to a true description of God as possible, knowing we will always fall short to some extent.

There are many descriptive statements which might be made about God, but it will be sufficient for this development to consider the following four aspects of God.

1 - God is All That Is, Everything. There is nothing that is not God.

2 - God is Mind, Thoughts, Ideas and nothing but Mind.

3 - God is Pure Love. All experiences of God are Loving.

4 - God Creates. God is not static, but is in a constant state of Creating.

If there were complete acceptance and belief in these four aspects, there would be nothing for us to learn. The purpose of this philosophy is to help us discover the barriers which prevent us from believing these ideas and to teach us how to remove those barriers.

1 – God is All That Is, Everything

Rather than just being omnipresent, in this philosophy God *is* everything. Nothing exists outside of God. If we believe we are experiencing something which is not God, we are simply fooling ourselves. Specifically this means the belief we are bodies or souls living in this world, and God is an entity outside of us, is an illusion.

2 – God is Mind

One of the more radical concepts in this philosophy is that God is only Mind. The only true experiences are ideas in the Mind of God, and since only Mind is real, anything material, physical, corporeal, etc. must be an illusion. The entire physical world with all of its complexity is just an illusory thought, and if we believe something is solid, permanent, or objective, we are deluding ourselves. In this philosophy everything happens in our minds, and any change we want to see must take place in our minds.

3 – God is Pure Love

In our world it is difficult to imagine an experience of Pure Love, but it is fundamental to the philosophy that God is only Love. If we think we are experiencing a God which is in any way less than a Loving God, then that 'God' is another illusion. We will see how in this philosophy one of the barriers to the experience of God is to see a 'God' that is not Loving. A 'God' that is judgmental, punishing, or merely too remote and abstract to experience is not a Loving God and must be illusory.

4 – God Creates

It is important not to see God as a static experience. God is the Source of our being – our True Self is God's creation, and this creation takes place in the Mind of God, which is the only place it can happen. Once created, this Self is fundamentally a co-creator extending the experience of God. Those creations occur in the Mind of God and therefore only exist and are only experienced in the Mind of God.

So why do we experience in our everyday lives something so different from this Natural State of Being? How is it possible we experience something other than Love? How can we possibly experience pain and attack or guilt and fear? All of these can be traced to our belief in the idea of separation.

The Idea of Separation

Having described the four aspects of God, we are now looking for a logical development which will lead us to better understand how we got to our current state of being from our Natural State. It is only necessary to find a single such development which can describe our current experience. The key fact is all of this is taking place within the mind, which allows for great freedom.

Suppose for a moment there was a thought of being separate from God. If the Mind of God *is* Everything, how can the thought of being separate from God exist? Since God is Creative, any thoughts are possible and free to be explored, so in some small corner, the illusory thought of separation is possible. But can a part of God's Mind actually separate from the Mind of God? In reality it cannot, but that does not mean the idea of separation and all of the possibilities it would entail cannot be explored. This is where we find ourselves.

Once the thought of separation occurs, the next question is, How would such a separation manifest itself and what would the experience be like? The first realization is that in order for any part of God to believe it has separated from God, it must delude itself, since real separation is impossible. How might such a delusion be formed?

Denying God

First the experience of God would have to be avoided, since this experience would break the spell of the belief in separation. One way to do this would be to introduce the idea of fear and the idea of something to be feared. In this scenario, God would become the focus of the fear; for if we do not fear God and were to re-experience the God of Pure Love, the illusion of separation would fall apart.

One way to create a fear of God is to see this new 'God' as an enemy who is out to harm us in some way, perhaps by judging us and potentially wanting to punish us for what we have done. This may sound preposterous, since God, by definition, is Pure Love, but it shows how absurd the idea of separation is and how much must be done to prop it up. If God were considered a friendly presence, the attraction to re-experience the Loving God would be too strong.

The Philosophy

The Separated Self

So an illusion has been created which essentially creates a ring around those thoughts of separation. Within the ring, all the thoughts are focused on seeing what is outside the ring as dangerous and fearful – an enemy. To reiterate, the ring, the fear, the enemy, are all imagined and have no basis in truth, and can only maintain their illusory state by constant effort to see something which is not there. The thoughts within the ring we will call the separated self.

Now suppose this scenario has been played out and a new separated self has been created. Of course, there really is no separated self, but there is a belief it has been created. This self will live in a state of fear, loneliness, and guilt for having cut itself off from what was its Natural Loving State of Being.

This state creates a great tension between the misery of the separated state and the nearness of God. The separated self will want to distance itself from this misery by building new barriers, new thoughts and ideas to focus on which will help it forget its true Natural State. One way the self can do this is to create within the ring the illusion of a separate external world, onto which it can project all of its guilt, pain, and fear.

The Separate External World

This external world is another construct of ideas, but the separated self can now believe it is real, a place where the self sees attacks occurring, along with pain and fear. Of course, all of this pain is being projected by the self onto the world, and is then being perceived as external to the self.

At this point the separated self can create the illusion of countless other separated selves, all existing in this projected world, all interacting with one another, and all projecting their thoughts out onto the world. The self can now be free of responsibility for the original thought of separation and allow the blame to be externalized. This has the additional benefit of creating a further layer of separation from God and the experience of Love.

The separated self can see itself as a lone bit of sanity in an insane external world – a world where the experience of love is fleeting, where death is always waiting, where attack, whether physical or emotional, is always present. By focusing on this world and learning how to defend itself from all these attacks, the memory of the Natural State fades further away. Of course, all of this is one great illusion, but the separated self will do what it must to maintain the idea of separation.

Since the separated self has created the external world to be a place of fear and attack, whenever this self interacts with this world, it will experience exactly what it projects onto that world. As the self further learns to project and then interact with the world, it begins to see the external world as its home. It becomes dependent on that world for its life and its sustenance. It begins to build up defenses to the attacks which are, by definition, part of that world – the world which is a completely delusional projection.

When discussing this separated self, it is important to understand that this self does not represent a person or a soul or any other of our common ideas of what a self is. Here the separated self is simply a construct of illusions that created the ring that separates these thoughts from the Oneness of the true Mind of God. The ring is not real and the idea of a separated self which can experience pain and guilt and fear is not real. But for the separated self, the illusion seems real, the external world seems real, and the pain and guilt and fear seem real.

For the remainder of the discussion, we will refer to the part of the separated self which focuses on maintaining the separation as the 'ego'. Later we will find there is another part of this separated self still connected to its Source which offers an alternative to the ego.

The Ego

The ego is the part of the separated self which focuses solely on the maintenance of the belief in separation. So what methods might the ego use to further the sense of separation and aloneness of the separated self? Most importantly, the ego must use whatever it can, especially guilt and fear, to prevent the separated self from remembering its connection to God. One of the ways it can maintain this belief is to try to keep the separated self focused on an external world.

The World Outside

One of the ego's goals is to create a solid feeling of self, of being an isolated individual living in an external objective world. The world we experience is a projection of the ego. The ego imagines guilt, fear, and attack and creates a complete external world which contains all of the same guilt, fear, and attack. The self then perceives this world as external and must use its focus and energies interacting with this world as if it was completely separate, when in reality it is its own projection.

The people we interact with, nature in all of its power and uncertainty, our activities, jobs, and creative work are all part of this ego construction, an illusion we have accepted without question. In order to interact with this projected world, the ego takes it one step further and constructs and maintains the illusion of a body.

The Body

As part of this illusion the ego creates a body with a precise sense of inside and outside. Within the body we appear to be at the mercy of our internal metabolic processes while from outside the body we are at the mercy of external forces. We spend, at the ego's request, a tremendous amount of our time building up defenses for our bodies. We build houses and other spaces to live, work, and play in. We procure and prepare sustenance for our bodies. The goal is to prolong the body in what we define (really what the ego defines) as a healthy state.

But lurking in our future is some kind of sickness, and that sickness may be generated internally in the body or it may be the result of some external agent which causes the sickness. Once we are sick, we must find external solutions to combat the sickness, and the ego tells us if we just take the right medicine or have the particular surgery or other procedure, we can return our bodies to health. But when we are old or too sick to keep our bodies going, we believe death will be the final chapter.

The Idea of Death

The ego has created an even greater idea to focus the energies of the self away from God – the idea of death. Everyone learns from an early age their bodies and other bodies are all going to die eventually. Our societies exert great effort and resources to prolong the life of the body to put off death as long as possible. But we also know death could occur in the next instant, and therefore we as bodies are never secure in this world. Given that experience, how could we imagine there was a Loving God who put us and our bodies in this world?

Then what is death? The answer lies in understanding what it is that is dying. When we examine human death, the only thing we are sure is dying is the human body. But the body is a creation of the ego, which is a part of the separated self. So the death of a body is only the death of an illusion – an illusion the ego has created to try to trap the separated self in this external world. In our philosophy, the Mind of God is Eternal and the Mind of God is Everything, so no matter how compelling it may seem, death is just another illusion created by the ego.

Hiding From God

As was mentioned, it is essential to the ego that we do not re-experience our existence within the Mind of God. God must be feared and we must feel deep guilt about our fear of God. There are basically two belief systems that exist in our world. One denies the existence of God, and for those who believe this, the world is a place of chance and chaos. One never knows what nature may inflict upon the self in this world – earthquakes, job loss, a car accident, loss of a friend, or perhaps the asteroid that hits the earth. This means the self must be in a constant state of fear. The fear may be deeply hidden and the external personality may be bright, but the ego-driven actions the self takes will be centered on how to maintain the body in this uncertain world.

The second basic belief, which pervades almost all religions to some extent, is the idea of God as a judgmental entity. In this scenario there is usually a concept of a life after death, and what that life is like is a result of what we do while we are here. Once again the ego creates a 'God' that is not Pure Love and we must be in fear of that 'God' because our future is in its hands. Since we can never live the life completely we are told we should (told by the ego, of course), we are constantly feeling guilty knowing we are offending this 'God'.

In both of these scenarios, the True God is hidden, and the fact this whole construction is a total illusion is obscured. If we can just go back to before the separation, there was and is nothing but the Mind of God, and all of the ego's manipulations are focused on maintaining the forgetting. As we will see later, there are ways to start to remember who and what we really are, ways which will ignore what the ego tells us is true and allow us to begin to see what is really there.

Judgment

Another tool the ego uses to focus the separated self on the external world is judgment. When we see this world from the ego's dualistic point of view, we are constantly judging the experiences, people, and ideas of this world. Fundamentally everything is looked at as to whether it increases pain or pleasure, and the mere process of judging means we have accepted the dualism of the ego. Therefore judgment helps to perpetuate the ego.

When we interact with people, we use judgment constantly to determine who can be our friends, who shares our politics, who we can love, who we can hate, who we need to fear. As we do this we place people in specific categories and by so doing we separate some people from others, leading to a strengthening of the idea of separation. The ego wants us to judge others and it also wants us to fear judgment from others. Through this process we lock ourselves deeper into this illusory world.

There are two fundamental lessons to be learned here. The first is to recognize how the ego operates in our lives as it projects onto the world all of our internal guilt, fear, and pain. In recognizing the actions of the ego, we begin to see the barriers that prevent us from experiencing the Love of God. The second lesson is to learn how to break through these barriers by practicing forgiveness.

Forgiveness

In this development we started with the four aspects of God. We then explored how a world like our current experience might have evolved, which led to the concept of separation, a mental construct of illusory ideas. We defined the ringed off set of ideas as the separated self, and the ego as the portion of the separated self focused on maintaining the separation. We examined how the ego creates the illusion of our separate external world, with our bodies inhabiting that world, and the many ways the ego maintains the illusion.

We now want to look at the part of the separated self that remembers the Natural State within the Mind of God. The ego wants to suppress that memory any way it can, but the memory is there nonetheless. We are offered the idea of forgiveness as a way to break the hold of the ego and to let the memory come to the surface. By forgiving the world we perceive, we will begin the journey back to God.

What Is Forgiveness?

In common usage forgiveness means to give up resentment toward someone or something. The word is used often in religious thought, but can also be used as a psychological term. In either case the resentment is seen as detrimental, and forgiveness will free us from those feelings. The term is most often used in regard to forgiving another person for some attack on oneself, whether physical, psychological, or emotional. In any case the assumption is the attack did occur and you are simply letting go of your resentment toward the person who attacked you.

In this philosophy, forgiveness has a very different and specific meaning and a unique power. Remember we began with our True Existence in the Mind of God. All else is illusion, including the separated self and the world in which that self believes it is living. If this is all an illusion, then any attack on this self must be an illusion as well. The ego wants us to see the attack as real, but if we can realize it is an illusion, the attack has no power against the self. This is what we mean by forgiveness – realizing the attack never really happened. In essence we forgive our perception of the event, which by extension forgives the person as well. The ego has projected the world we perceive, so as we forgive the world around us, we weaken the power of the ego.

It is important to realize the word attack is used in a very general sense and there are no degrees of attack. Being physically attacked is just the same as someone saying an unkind word about you, or a politician wanting to raise your taxes or take away your benefits, or your boss demanding something from you. In all these cases the ego has projected an experience which is not perceived as loving, and in all these cases forgiveness can free your perception of the experience and allow you to realize the ego was fooling you again. It doesn't matter where you begin your forgiveness, it only matters that you apply it to everything. If you withhold forgiveness for any one thing, the ego has maintained its illusion of separation.

Loving and Non-Loving Thoughts

In learning how to forgive, we will have to choose what we are going to forgive. Since the change we want to occur must happen within the mind, ultimately what we will always be forgiving are our thoughts. Those thoughts may contain emotions and memories of events and people involved in those events, but it is the thoughts which will be forgiven, and in the process the events and people, including ourselves, will be forgiven as well.

In order to choose which thoughts to forgive, there is a simple test we can use. Is the thought a loving or a non-loving thought? If it is a kind, loving, caring, compassionate thought, there is no need for forgiveness, since the experience of Love is our Natural State. If it is non-loving, a thought of anger, pain, attack, fear, guilt, depression, hatred, conditional 'love', sadness, grief, etc., then that thought is a misperception of the world and who we are, and is ripe for forgiveness.

As we will discuss in detail later, most of our everyday thoughts are non-loving ones, for these are the thoughts the ego uses to help it maintain our belief in the idea of separation. Each of us therefore will find plenty of material within our own minds to which we can apply forgiveness. The starting point for practicing forgiveness is to recognize our own non-loving thoughts.

The Inner Spirit and Forgiveness

Of course it's not always going to be easy to forgive. The mere fact we perceive ourselves as bodies living in an external world means we have given a great deal of power to the ego, whose sole reason for being is to maintain the separation. We said earlier there is another part of the separated self that remembers the Mind of God. We will refer to this part as the Inner Spirit.

The Inner Spirit might be seen within our minds as a personality or a larger than life spiritual entity, our connection to God. We observe this entity as the part of the mind that remembers our True Existence. The process of forgiving an attack starts with recognizing we have perceived an attack occurring in the external world. We then take the thought of that attack, and knowing that to the Inner Spirit the attack could never have occurred, we hand off to the Inner Spirit all of our feelings about the attack, and by doing so we free ourselves of these feelings.

A more visual and less personal way to think of the Inner Spirit is as a tunnel which opens out from the ego's world through the ego's barriers and through the outer ring into the True Mind of God. It's a mental path through which we access our Natural State. By envisioning this tunnel we can again hand off the pain, guilt, and fear we experience in the ego's world, so it can be sucked into the tunnel to disappear into the Mind of God. What is happening when we do this is we are for a brief moment remembering where we came from, and by doing so we are forgiving the experience which led to our feelings of attack.

What Else Can We Forgive?

We have been focusing on forgiveness in the context of forgiving another person for a perceived attack. When we use this method of forgiveness, we are really forgiving the experience of the attack. By extension the person who we believed attacked us in the first place is also forgiven, since if the attack did not occur, the person did not commit the attack.

We can extend this idea of forgiveness to any non-loving thought, including internal guilt about acts we believe we have committed in the past, illnesses which may appear to have come from within the body or from an outside agent, the fears we have about attacks which could occur in the future, and our judgments and the judgments of others. And of course there is also the fear and guilt we feel about our initial rejection of the Loving God and our replacement with the ego's concept of the judgmental 'God' or the non-existent God.

Guilt and Fear of God

Some of the deepest guilt and fear we experience are related to our feelings about God. Remember the whole idea of separation started with our rejection of the Loving God and the creation of a judgmental, punishing 'God', or the belief there is no God. In either case we have substituted our Loving place in the Mind of God with a non-loving experience in this world, which has led to deep pain, guilt, and fear. We must forgive our guilt for believing we left God and our fear of some kind of retribution from the judgmental 'God'. The Inner Spirit stands ready to help us heal these feelings as well. First we must recognize our part in creating this illusion and then release those feelings to the Inner Spirit to remember again our Existence in the Loving Mind of God.

The Way Home

We began our philosophy with the four aspects of God. These aspects define our Natural State of Being. Then the idea of separation occurred, which is just an illusion, but the idea led to the ringed off separated self, another illusion. We defined the ego as the part of the separated self that maintains the illusion of separation. We explored the different ways the ego works to maintain the illusion. We then learned about forgiveness and how through forgiveness we can begin to break the hold of the ego. With the help of the Inner Spirit, the part of the separated self that remembers its Natural State, we free ourselves of the pain, guilt, and fear in our lives.

The first part of the development of the philosophy is focused on understanding how we got where we are and how we maintain our current separated state. Through this understanding we can begin to recognize the actions of the ego. Once recognition has occurred, we begin to forgive all the non-loving thoughts existing within our minds. Through this process of forgiveness, we are letting go, step by step, of the separation illusion, and we will remember more and more our Natural Existence in the Mind of God.

Peace

So where does all of this lead? The goal of this philosophy is to experience Peace. What do we mean by Peace? In essence it is a state of continual forgiveness, living your life with a constant realization the world we inhabit is an illusion and is not our True Home. As events occur, they are instantly seen as illusions, instantly forgiven, and any negative feelings are passed on to the Inner Spirit. By continually forgiving our experiences in this world, the ego is no longer in charge of the separated self. The pain, guilt, and fear which are normally experienced are forgiven and this new self identifies more and more with the Inner Spirit. The remembrance of the True Natural State becomes ever stronger.

How can we experience this Peace? As with many things we learn in this world, through constant practice. The ego is a strong force and before learning this philosophy we spent much of our lives believing the ego's view of the world, a place of fear and attack from which we must protect ourselves. Once we open ourselves to an awareness of the Inner Spirit's presence, we can begin the process of breaking down all of the ego's barriers – all of the guilt and fear we have accepted from the ego throughout our lives.

Through the experience of the Inner Spirit, we can begin to remember on a daily basis our True Existence in the Mind of God. Eventually that daily remembrance can become a constant remembrance and a state of continual forgiveness can be achieved. Peace can be ours whether our bodies continue to inhabit this world or not. Once forgiveness is a constant practice, and Peace becomes our everyday experience, there is nothing in the world that can take this from us. Our Peace is our own and any attack on that Peace is just a fleeting illusion which will instantly die away.

The End of Illusion

There will come a time when this world of illusion and separation will be gone. Everything we currently experience – past, present, and future – will disappear. Once we find our way back to the Loving Mind of God, all of the illusions that have grabbed our focus will fade away. The separated self and the ring that encloses it, the ego and all of its tricks, our external world and all of the bodies in that world, even the Inner Spirit who helped lead us out of the illusion – all of these will be gone and we will live in a state of Love and Peace and Creation unimaginable to us where we are now.

The purpose of this book is to teach you how to forgive, and how to make forgiveness a regular practice. In the next chapters we will go through the process step by step with the goal of making forgiveness the most natural thing you can do. Through practicing forgiveness, you will be fundamentally changing your life, seeing the world around you in an entirely different light. No longer must you live with fear and guilt, for this practice will free you to be your True Self.

Making a List

We have now presented a new philosophy, a reality built around the Loving Mind of God, our Natural State of Being. Within that State, we have tremendous freedom to explore and create, and one of those explorations has taken us down the path of the idea of separation. We have created an illusory world we have focused on to the exclusion of everything else. Within this world the ego has dominated our thoughts. But by realizing the illusion of what we are seeing through forgiveness, we have a path back to the Loving Place which is our True Home.

In this book, we are going to learn a simple three-step process for forgiveness. The first step in the process is to choose something to forgive. This may seem fairly obvious to you, but within this philosophy, you will find there are likely many more things you can forgive than you first thought. We will be forgiving the big things in your life, but we will also be forgiving many little things, because everything which is not leading you closer to love is a barrier you need to remove.

As a starting point for learning to practice forgiveness, we will begin with the idea of loving and non-loving thoughts. You will learn to recognize these types of thoughts within your own mind, and once you do, you will be taking the first step in understanding this way of forgiveness. Everything you need is within your mind – your thoughts, memories, and emotions. With these, you have the raw material necessary to change your world through forgiveness.

Loving Thoughts

There is a loving side to each of us. This loving part is the core of who we are, the part that connects us with the Loving Mind of

God. This love is unconditional love, feelings of kindness and compassion toward a person, or a group of people, with no expectation of anything in return. When we are in this place of unconditional love, everything in the world seems to shine with an extraordinary light. For most people, these moments are fleeting and these thoughts will soon be replaced by our more ordinary, less loving thoughts.

> "I was attending a musical performance with a friend. As I walked into the auditorium, I began to feel an incredible connection to everyone there. It was as if I was in love with every person attending the event. I didn't say anything to my friend about this, nor do I think I could have said anything. It was just so wonderful, I knew it was beyond words. For the next half-hour or so, I basked in this feeling of love and light, and then just as mysteriously as it had begun, it faded away and the world was normal again."

It is important to understand the unconditional nature of this love. We say we love many things and many people in this life, but most of our relationships have some conditions to them. We expect something from those we love. We want them to love us as much as we love them. We want them to express this love by acting in certain ways. If they fail to act as we wish, something will feel wrong about our shared love. We might want to talk to them and see if we can work things out, the things we are both setting as conditions.

True unconditional love has none of this. With no conditions, the love we express comes with no expectations of anything in return. This is the place we are heading in this book – an experience where only love is expressed to everyone we come in contact with, an experience where the world is felt as a place of peace and hope and oneness. Once we let go of the idea of separation, there will be nothing left but love. This book will start you on the path to this loving, peaceful experience. By following the practice of forgiveness, you will transform your life to one of True Love.

However, at this point we will stop talking about unconditional love, the experience of oneness with everyone. For this book is not about seeking love, for that love is already our Natural State. This book is about removing the barriers to love. In order to remove those barriers, we need to recognize what they are. Once we recognize a barrier, we will apply forgiveness and will miraculously see it disappear. We will then go on to the next barrier and the next. These barriers are our non-loving thoughts.

Non-Loving Thoughts

What is a non-loving thought? It is any thought other than the loving, kind, compassionate, caring thoughts that grow out of unconditional love. This means our everyday lives are dominated by non-loving thoughts. If you feel anger toward someone, if you are fearful of someone or something, if you feel guilty about something, all of these are examples of non-loving thoughts. By believing we live in this world, we will all have these non-loving thoughts on a daily basis, and these thoughts will often have strong emotions associated with them. The emotions and the thoughts go together, and part of the process of forgiving them will include experiencing these emotions as completely as possible.

Non-loving thoughts also include more than just these strong negative emotions. They can be seemingly neutral as well. The thought that we are a body living in the physical world seems relatively neutral, but it is a non-loving thought because that belief stands between us and the realization of our Oneness with the Loving God. Any such thought is an ego thought and therefore is a non-loving thought, since the ego's purpose is to hide love from us by building the barriers to love. It is the ego that fills our heads with non-loving thoughts and most of the time we choose to listen.

These non-loving thoughts are more than just a minor annoyance in our otherwise normal life. These thoughts are what form the life we believe we are living here, our life as a body living in a physical world. If we could somehow miraculously remove all the non-loving thoughts from our minds, this world and everything in it would disappear and we would reconnect with our True Self. It is our constant choice to focus on these thoughts which binds us to this world.

In this philosophy, everything happens in the mind, and only through understanding how our minds work do we have the opportunity to change our lives. If we want more love in our lives, we must remove these barriers, these non-loving thoughts from our minds. Once we do, the Loving Self who we really are will shine through and simple love will rise to the surface. Recognition of non-loving thoughts is the first step on the road to Peace.

Once you begin to recognize your non-loving thoughts, you can begin to apply the practice of forgiveness to the thoughts. This is the sole purpose of forgiveness – to ultimately free your mind from non-loving thoughts. You will begin to see you have a choice in every moment to accept and embrace these thoughts, or to release them through forgiveness. If you release them, the ego will lose its power over you and you will naturally become a more kind, compassionate, and loving person.

Now let's look as some specific examples of non-loving thoughts. You should be able to recognize thoughts in your own mind which are similar to these examples. The most important thing in learning to forgive is to first look inside your mind and find the thoughts that need forgiveness.

Some Types of Non-Loving Thoughts

- Anger

All of us get angry at one time or another. It may have happened already today, or in the last few days. You may be in a peaceful place for a while, but then something will happen which will really get you riled. You want to lash out however you can and let that other person know what they did was wrong. You want that person to feel guilty about what they did. This is the essence of anger – trying to make someone else feel guilty for what they have done.

> "My sister, Sheila, and I had a big fight about something she said. There was a lot of yelling and I slammed the door when I left. Sometimes I can't believe the way she acts. I love her, but I get so angry with her."

Anger can be very personal, and in fact, often our strongest feelings of anger are toward ones we say we love, like family and friends and spouses. We have expectations from them, and want them to feel guilty when they do something that falls short of our expectations. But anger can also be toward strangers. We get angry at politicians, at criminals, at anyone who fails to live up to a certain standard, a standard we believe in. These standards and expectations are the ego's tools for keeping us focused on how we are separate from those around us.

Our religions, philosophies, and psychologies teach us many different ways to deal with our anger. In some we are told to suppress our anger, to hide it inside so we won't hurt anyone by expressing it. The anger is still there waiting for another opportunity to come out. In others we are told we must express the anger to free ourselves, an expression which often ignores the feelings of the person we are angry with. No matter where anger appears to come from and no matter whether we express it or not, anger is always a tool of the ego, a non-loving thought we can choose to forgive.

- *Fear*

Fear seems to be a basic part of who we are. When we view ourselves through an evolutionary lens, in our distant past we were both the hunter and the hunted. We were hunted by predators and by our human enemies. It is small wonder we seem to be fearful from the time we are born. The things we are afraid of will change as we go through the stages of life, and people in different social and economic situations will have different fears.

> "Sheila is coming over here tomorrow. I'm so worried about how she is going to treat me, and I'm worried I won't be able to control myself if she treats me the way she usually does. I wonder if there is some way I can avoid her."

Fundamentally we fear something that might happen in the future. In most cases what we fear never comes to pass, so we end up expending a great deal of emotional and mental energy on worry about what will not occur. Once again this fear is a tool of the ego. When we fear those around us, we are expressing our belief in the idea of separation. We see the differences in these others, and fear the differences may lead to some attack on us, whether verbal or physical.

It is impossible to love someone we fear. The fear blinds us to the true guiltless nature of the other person. The fear requires we create defenses so these attacks will not occur. This means fear is at its core a non-loving thought, a way for the ego to keep us trapped in this illusion. Only through forgiveness can we free ourselves from fear.

- Guilt

In our world, there is external guilt and internal guilt. We see people doing things we know are wrong and judge them guilty. These may be strangers committing crimes or family members hurting one another. We know there is a justice system that will punish the guilty who commit crimes. For the more personal hurts, we must rely on blame and anger to express our feelings.

There is also internal guilt, feelings we have about the things we know we have done wrong in our lives. These are all the hurts, small and large, we have inflicted on others even though we try to be good as much as possible. Sometimes we just can't seem to help it, and sometimes things seem out of our control. The result is our own guilt, which we do our best to hide from others.

> "I feel really bad about yelling at Sheila. I know she deserved it for some of the things she said, but I shouldn't have just thrown it back at her. I should be better than that, but I'm not."

Every one of these instances of guilt is a non-loving thought. Remember your True Self is at one with the Mind of God. This God is only Loving, so this Self cannot be guilty of anything. It is the ego that tells us we are guilty and it is the ego that projects this guilt out onto the world for us to perceive. When we perceive it, we then feel we can judge these others, these separate others, for what they have done. These ego-generated non-loving thoughts are ready for forgiveness.

- Conditional Love

When we love someone conditionally, it is not really love at all. It may feel like love, but eventually some need will not be met and this conditional love will fail. A way to test if your feelings of love are conditional would be to imagine if the other person left you or acted badly toward you. Would you feel the same love toward them, a love without sadness or anger?

"I really do love Sheila, but I would love her so much more if she would only treat me better. Why won't she see how good I can be instead of always seeing my faults?"

Unconditional love is the only real love in this philosophy. It's possible to feel kindness and compassion toward someone without ever expecting anything in return. Everyone has the capacity for this unconditional love, but the ego wants to hide this capacity from us. The ego wants us to see faults in others so we can express anger and disappointment in them, even though we seem to care for them.

Through forgiveness, it is ultimately possible for us to express only unconditional love. We will see later how we can reach a state where we see everyone around us as one with us, and not separate. We can reach a state of peace where the buffeting events of our everyday lives have no effect on our state of being. This is the promise of forgiveness leading to a life of unconditional love.

- Grief

Grief is fundamentally a feeling of loss, the feeling one gets when someone or something is taken away, whether through death or in other ways. This can include illness, ending a relationship, or losing a job. Grief is considered a natural reaction to loss, a way for us to process these events in our lives and to move on to some kind of closure.

"Sheila wrote me a letter saying she didn't want to see me anymore. I can't believe she would cut me off like that. I feel so sad that she won't be part of my life."

Of course, the most profound grief we feel is when someone close to us dies. What we saw as a vital human being interacting with us and the rest of this world is now a lifeless shell. We can no longer talk to this person, no longer touch this person, and this seems to leave a big hole in our lives. Our perception of death causes us to feel sadness, grief, and sometimes anger.

But this perception of loss is just another tool of the ego. We can only lose something which is separate from us. As long as we see others as bodies living in the external world, we will at times lose these bodies. But these bodies are part of the ego's illusion of separation. If we can realize through forgiveness we are not separate from anyone, then grief can be seen as another ego illusion.

- Depression

Depression is characterized by low mood, low self-worth, and disinterest in the normal activities of life. Whether depression is an illness or a psychological problem is irrelevant in this philosophy. The body is an illusory projection of the ego and hence any illness in that body will also be such a projection. This means all illness, psychological or otherwise, originates in the mind. In our discussions, depression is therefore always a mental issue, as are all other non-loving thoughts.

Some individuals seem to deal with depression for much of their lives, while for others, depression results from unpleasant events in life. Feelings of guilt, grief, and fear can lead to feelings of helplessness and low self-worth. This can spiral into obsessive focus on the negative thoughts in one's mind.

> "I don't know what to do about the situation with Sheila. It seems like I have these problems with everybody in my life. What's wrong with me? I just don't feel like I can cope anymore."

Feelings of low self-worth are clearly non-loving thoughts toward oneself. If we feel we are bad or something is wrong with us, then we are not loving ourselves. The ego wants us to feel bad, for the ego knows that as long as we are focused on what's wrong, we will be unable to see what's right. These non-loving thoughts can be forgiven like all non-loving thoughts, and we can discover our true self-worth, which is our connection to the Loving Mind of God.

Making a List

Now that you have an understanding of non-loving thoughts, you should be able to recognize these thoughts within your mind. The next step is to make a list of these thoughts you can use to apply to the process of forgiveness. This list will be your starting point when you take some quiet time during the day to practice forgiveness. This list contains the thoughts which are the barriers to the experience of love in your life. This list and the application of forgiveness to it has the potential to radically change your life.

The list can be written down on paper or in a notebook. It can be typed into a computer, smartphone, or other device. What is important is that it is put into some physical form and is not just something you try to keep in your memory. You can set aside some time each day to add items to the list, or you can keep the list with you and add items as they occur to you, or both. There is no right way to create your list; it is only important you create one and add your non-loving thoughts to it.

Each item on the list should have a separate line and should be described in about 20 words or less. Remember this list is just for you and is really a way for you to jog your memory about a thought you had. You should leave a space in front of the item to put a checkmark or an 'x' or some other notation you will place there when you have completed the process of forgiveness for that item. The idea is once you start the list, you do not remove items from the list, but simply check off the ones you have taken care of. This way you can go back at a later time and see the results of your practice.

So what non-loving thoughts should we include on the list? The easiest way to start for most people is to remember some events from the last few days which are fresh in your mind. We all should be able to come up with some examples recently where we have felt anger, fear, guilt, pain, sadness, etc. As you read this section, this might be a good time to start your list. Just grab whatever is convenient for you and write down your first few items. This will give you something to work with as we proceed. As an example,

"Sheila was so mean to me the other day, I just wanted to scream."

The next time you approach your list you may want to search further in your past, say the last five years or so, for events that invoke non-loving thoughts. Write some of these down, and then go back ten years or fifteen to find some other thoughts. Once you have a few of these, think about some of the things you fear about the future. Are you worried about some criminal attack that may befall you? Are you worried about something happening to your family members? Are you worried about wars and the world situation? These fears are all non-loving thoughts which can be forgiven. For example,

"There's so much crime in our neighborhood right now, I worry about being safe."

"I'm so afraid for our soldiers fighting in the war."

Are there things you feel guilty about? Have you said things to someone or acted in a way you regret? These feelings of guilt are certainly not loving toward yourself and should be added to the list. If you hear about criminal acts that have been committed and you want that person to feel guilty, this is another non-loving thought. If you have been angry with someone, it is likely because you wanted them to take responsibility for something they did to you and you wanted them to feel guilty. Some examples,

"I feel guilty about yelling at Sheila the other day."

"That murderer I saw on TV is certainly guilty."

As you begin this process you will most likely find there are far more thoughts than you actually want to write down. Don't worry about trying to write down every non-loving thought you have ever had. Just make a reasonable list of items, one that will give you adequate material for practicing forgiveness. You can always add more items at a later time. What is important is that you don't reject a thought because it's too awful or the emotions are too raw. Try to view each event or thought as objectively as you can. The emotions can be dealt with later as we continue to practice forgiveness.

Finally, there should not be any order to the list. Don't try to group the items or insert items into a particular position. Simply add the next thought you want to add to the bottom of the list. This means items from the past, present, and future will be intermixed. Items of anger, fear, sadness, and conditional love will be randomly placed on the list. When you choose items from the list, this randomness will make it less likely you will reject certain types of non-loving thoughts, and you will therefore be more open to applying forgiveness to everything.

So now before we proceed further, take a moment and use whatever is at hand – paper, your computer, your phone – and start your list. Simply choose an event from your recent days which had negative emotions attached to it, a non-loving thought, and write the item down. Now you have started your list and now you are ready to learn how to forgive. If you have a little time right now, add a few more items to the list. Think about a time later in the day, maybe at lunch or after dinner, when you can set aside a few minutes to add to the list. Once the first items are on the list, the process has begun.

Choosing from the List

We'll discover in the chapter 'How to Practice Forgiveness' that the first step in forgiving is to choose something to forgive. This is the purpose of our list. Depending on how diligently you work at making your list, you might have twenty items or you might have hundreds. The question will arise as to which item you should forgive next. You might pick the first item on the list, or the last, or you might close your eyes and place your finger on the list and see where it lands. It actually doesn't matter what you choose, except you should never consciously reject an item because it seems too bad or too big and scary.

The more randomly you choose, the better. Within the randomness lies the chance for your subconscious to help you in your choice. The randomness also helps eliminate any bias you have about certain thoughts you have had. In the beginning, this will help guide you to making the right decisions about what to forgive. As time goes on and you feel more comfortable with the process, you may not need the list as much and can rely on your own internal awareness of non-loving thoughts to guide you. The list is here to get you started down the path, a path that can lead to fundamental change in your life.

Once you have applied forgiveness to one of these items, you will put a check or an 'x' in front of it to indicate you have forgiven it. Over time your list will become a mix of checked and unchecked items. As you go back and read these items, you may find there is much more emotional content lingering in the unchecked items. There should be a feeling of freedom about the checked items, as if they have been cleansed. This is the purpose of forgiveness – to cleanse the non-loving thoughts from our minds leaving only love.

Now before you begin to learn the full process of forgiveness, you must first learn about the Inner Spirit. An essential part of this philosophy is that you do not have to practice forgiveness all on your own. You have all the help you need once you make a commitment to wanting to change. All you need is a little willingness and from that you will be guided along the process. In the next chapter you will learn about the Inner Spirit and ways to connect with this Inner Spirit within your mind. Once you understand how to make this connection, you will be ready to tackle the first item from your list.

Finding the Inner Spirit

You now have learned what it is you are going to forgive, your non-loving thoughts. You have learned how to identify these thoughts, and have started to make a list you can refer to as you learn the steps to forgiveness. The second step in the process is to connect with your Inner Spirit, a critical part of achieving real forgiveness. This connection is of utmost importance to the process, since trying to forgive on your own without any help is extremely difficult. This is one of the reasons so many people fail when they try to forgive using a different method.

At this point you may not feel like you have any real connection to the Inner Spirit within you, and that is perfectly normal. You have spent your whole life listening primarily to the ego and have ignored the other side of yourself. In this chapter, we will explore the Inner Spirit, and discuss several techniques for bringing it more into awareness. Once you start down this path, you may wonder how you missed this part of yourself for all those years.

What Is the Inner Spirit?

One of the implications of the idea of separation is the illusion of a split mind. We believe, imagine, dream there is a part of the mind which is separate from God. This part is the ego, and as we live in this imagined world, we listen to the ego as we make our day-to-day decisions. We believe the ego has our best interests at heart, and we believe that without the ego, we would not be able to survive in this world. If we only listen to the ego, we cannot achieve complete forgiveness since forgiveness is the antidote to separation. Without complete forgiveness, we will continue to choose the ego's view of the world, the world of attack and guilt and fear we believe we live in.

If the ego is the part of the split mind that focuses on the separation, and if the separation is an illusion and we are not truly separate from God, there must be another part of the mind that can't see the separation, that sees only our Oneness within the Mind of God. That part we will call the Inner Spirit. It is important if you want to see beyond the ego's world that you find this part of your mind, this Inner Spirit, and an essential step in practicing forgiveness is getting in touch with the Inner Spirit.

So how do we find the Inner Spirit within? Where has it been hiding all these years? Why doesn't it just speak up so we can hear it? Is it just so ethereal we can never grasp hold of it?

In simplest terms, the Inner Spirit is the connection between the separated world we believe in and the Home within the Mind of God our True Self has never left. Since we believe so thoroughly in all the illusions the ego has presented to us, we need help in finding our way to forgiveness. The Inner Spirit offers that help and is always available to us. The Inner Spirit is where the only true fulfillment and happiness can be found, for it truly has your best interest in mind.

It knows we can only achieve peace and joy by remembering our connection to God, and through this connection we can begin to remember where it is we ultimately come from. This small remembrance is what will propel you forward to change the way you see the world. If you know deeply that you have another life beyond this world, a life within a Pure Loving Space, it will change your perspective on everything you do in this life. All you will need to get started is your willingness to find the Inner Spirit.

Your Willingness

The Inner Spirit asks only your small willingness, a simple intent to find another way. We are all weary in this world because we have listened to the ego for too long. Out of this weariness, we must search for new direction, the direction back to our Home in God, and the Inner Spirit is your path to that Home. This willingness will bring you the peace you desire.

Finding the Inner Spirit is not about searching, but about intending. When you make a clear intention, you will find what has always been waiting within your mind, for God intended you to find this path back Home. It's as if this willingness on your part turns on a light in your mind, and the love and peace you find in the direction of that light will act as a guide as you learn to truly forgive.

As you learn to forgive and put forgiveness into practice, you will on a daily basis be strengthening your connection to the Inner Spirit. You will more and more begin to follow the will of the Inner Spirit, a will that is the antithesis of the ego's willfulness. The will of the Inner Spirit always and forever knows what is best for you, and if you follow this will, you can find pure unconditional love in your everyday life. You will make decisions with the help of the Inner Spirit and no longer feel you are completely on your own. You will begin to weaken the ego's hold on you.

You have taken the first step toward true forgiveness by beginning your list of non-loving thoughts. The second step is a decision on your part, a decision to find the Inner Spirit, to show your willingness to find a better way. Once you show the willingness, the Inner Spirit promises to respond, and if you are open to the signs in your life, you will observe this response within your mind and in the world around you.

The Inner Spirit and Forgiveness

It is very important for you to realize that trying to forgive without a connection to God is a futile exercise. Through the Inner Spirit, we can find the connection and realize it's our Loving Place in the Pure Mind of God which makes forgiveness possible. As we will see in the next chapter, forgiveness is a process of seeing the illusions in life, and with our connection to the Inner Spirit, we have a means for letting those illusions go. Imagine what it would be like to try to forgive without a connection to God.

"I'm really going to try to forgive Sheila. I know she's been mean to me at times, but I have to be a better person than that. The next time I see her, I'm going to try to forget all the things she's done over the years and try to see her as just a loving person, who maybe doesn't know how to express it sometimes. Hopefully she'll see I'm trying to see her differently and she'll not be so mean."

So what is happening here? The first thing to notice is there seems to be a real effort required, saying words like 'try' and 'hopefully'. The second thing to notice is the belief Sheila really has been mean, that an attack has really occurred. Once there is an acceptance Sheila has attacked, the only thing that can be done is to 'try to forget', to see her differently even though the evidence hasn't shown she has changed. It's all just an exercise in hope and maybes.

Now let's consider how forgiveness can work when we are connected to the Inner Spirit. In the next chapter we will show in more detail the exact steps to take to achieve this way of forgiveness, but for now, following our basic philosophy and having found the Inner Spirit, it might go more like this.

"I'm going to forgive Sheila. I'll take all the non-loving thoughts I have about her and through my connection to God, through my Inner Spirit, I will see within my mind there's a place of Pure Love. Within that place of Love, no anger or guilt can exist, and these non-loving thoughts will be seen for what they are, the ego's illusions."

The first thing to note is there is no need for trying and hoping. If we have made the connection, we are assured that forgiveness will occur and we will be able to see the ego illusion. Secondly, there is no acknowledgment any attack has occurred. We are simply forgiving the non-loving thoughts in the mind. And finally, we must find the place of Love within the mind to truly experience the end to these illusory thoughts.

The advantages to having this connection become clear. With the connection, it matters not at all what happens in the external world. Everything we need to change our experience is within the mind, and most importantly, the path to God is within the mind. God is Mind and our True Self is a part of that Mind. By finding the Inner Spirit, we now have the possibility of a lifelong connection to the Mind of God. The power of this connection can bring peace and love into your life in a way you could never imagine before.

Now we are going to look for some techniques for reaching the Inner Spirit. In the beginning, these will all be some form of meditative practice, which can be very formalized or very freeform. Whatever you do, it starts with quieting the mind.

Quieting the Mind

The ego really likes noise. The noisier your mind and the noisier the world around you, the better the ego likes it. The 'monkey mind' is a popular term which refers to the seemingly endless monologues going on inside our heads. It's called the monkey mind, because like the activity of a monkey jumping from one thing to another, our thoughts seem to randomly jump around no matter how much we try to concentrate and control them.

For example, you might be simply walking along a quiet path and your mind will be thinking about almost everything except your immediate surroundings. Conversations you had earlier in the day, plans you have for later in the day – anything but what is going on in your present. It is this lack of focus on the present which is central to the working of the monkey mind.

What's important to understand in this philosophy is that the monkey mind is purposeful. It is a tool of the ego. It's not some random firing of synapses or some failure in our concentration abilities. It's the way the ego uses our chaotic thoughts to create the chaotic world we believe we see in front of us. This monkey mind is the ego at work, projecting thoughts and feelings out into the world for us to perceive.

It is the chaos of these thoughts which makes the world seem so dangerous and unpredictable. If we truly are projecting the world we see, then if we can change our thoughts away from the chaos, the world we experience will be less chaotic. Remember that achieving peace is our goal, and peace is in the mind. If we can stop listening to the ego and can realize attack and pain and guilt and fear are illusions, then we will discover the peace that was always there waiting.

Many spiritual traditions include some kind of contemplative activity. In Western religions these are more focused around prayer, a means through which we may communicate with God. In some of the more mystical sects, this includes deep meditation, but in general, the process of quieting the mind is not emphasized in the Western traditions.

The Eastern religions use meditation as a core element of the practice, and these practices include ways to calm the mind. The concept of the monkey mind or mind monkey comes from the Buddhist traditions of Eastern Asia. In Buddhism, one is urged to learn to retrain the mind through contemplation, to see the world as the illusion it is, and to achieve a state of peace. The ultimate goal is to awaken to enlightenment, an awareness of Nirvana, the state of Pure Being.

The practice of Yoga preceded the time of the Buddha by many centuries and meditation was a fundamental part of yogic practice. Today meditation is practiced in both of these traditions though there are subtle differences in approach, and some significant differences in the understanding of where the meditation is leading.

What is common is the practice of quieting the mind. In some forms of meditation, there is a mantra which is said over and over in order to focus the mind. In others there is only concentration on breathing, and in some, there is a focus on being completely in the present moment at all times. All of these states help to turn off the monkey mind, to bring the individual more completely into the present, and ultimately to achieve a state of peace.

In order to learn to practice forgiveness, it is essential we experience the Inner Spirit, and in order to do this, we must quiet our thoughts. Once we are in touch with the Inner Spirit, the full process of forgiveness can proceed. The plan is fairly simple. By setting aside some time every day, you have the chance to step away from the monkey mind and focus on what really matters. It doesn't matter how you do it, only that you do it consistently. You are showing the Inner Spirit your intent, and in changing your mind, intent is everything.

As part of this process of quieting the mind, you are going to focus away from your chaotic thoughts to the peaceful thought of the Inner Spirit. As you do, you are fundamentally changing the way you will interact with the world. Quieting the monkey mind frustrates the ego, since it is dependent on these chaotic thoughts for its existence. As you practice forgiveness, and take some quiet time each day, you will be on the path to a different life. In time, the peacefulness that is naturally yours will take over your mind, and will be reflected in the world around you.

We can begin to heal the distress and turmoil in our lives by realizing the ego and the monkey mind are one and the same. By quieting one, you are weakening the other. Make it your goal to live in the peace inside your mind. Make it your goal to turn off the monkey mind once and for all, and hear only the soft clear loving voice of the Inner Spirit.

At this point it is important to note that the ultimate goal is to be able to touch the Inner Spirit and practice forgiveness in all kinds of situations. It is clearly easier to do this when everything around you is quiet, but if that is the only time you are able to forgive, peace will never fully arrive for you. This means we will use the quiet time to learn the techniques, so that eventually we will be able to apply forgiveness in the most chaotic situations possible.

You may or may not have tried meditation before. If you have, and you have a technique that works for you, a technique that helps you quiet your mind, it might be easiest for you in the beginning to continue to follow that practice. Many meditative techniques have only the quieting of the mind as the goal. Over time, you will want to focus your meditations toward the Inner Spirit. Feeling the connection is crucial to the process of forgiveness.

If you have not meditated before, there is no magic required here, no chanting or gurus or charms. All that is required is to look inside your mind for the place of peace. It is there whether right now you believe it or not. The next section provides one simple technique for getting in touch with the Inner Spirit, a method you can use over and over whenever you need to practice forgiveness.

A Simple Meditative Technique

In this section we will show how you can connect to the Inner Spirit through a peaceful meditation. There are many different ways to envision the Inner Spirit, but we will explore a simple visual meditation as one means for contact. Though it may seem like you are just using your imagination in this exercise, it is important to remember the Inner Spirit is very real, more real than anything in your life.

Begin by sitting in a quiet place free of distractions. Get comfortable, close your eyes and take a few deep breaths. At this stage the only thing you need to do is to relax as much as possible. The relaxation allows your mind to begin to free itself from the ego's influence. Start with your feet and toes and work your way up the body relaxing each part until you reach the top of your head. Continue to breathe easily. In the beginning the process of relaxing may take some time, so don't feel rushed. Eventually as you do this regularly, you will be able to move to this quiet place more quickly.

Once you feel very relaxed, imagine your mind is a large space above and including your head. The space is huge, extending in all directions and without boundaries. Within this huge space, there are innumerable thoughts flying about. Focus on one of these thoughts for a second or two and then let it go. Focus on another and let it go. Do this for a minute or so and realize you have a choice of which thoughts you can focus on. This will allow you to choose the thoughts you want to be your focus.

Take a few moments to just feel this space, this mind that is your current experience. Now for awhile, try observing all the thoughts without fixating on anything. Just be aware of the motion. The thoughts are like a huge flock of birds flying around in all directions. These thoughts are overwhelmingly the result of the ego trying to maintain the idea of separation.

Now take your focus over to the left side of your mind, the left side of this huge space you are observing. Next imagine all the thoughts from this left side of your mind begin to migrate over to the right side. Slowly but steadily these busy thoughts, like the flying birds, move over to the right side of your mind. As this occurs, the right side becomes a hive of activity, thoughts of everything physical and emotional flying around. This wild motion is what your everyday thinking is like.

Continue this process for as long as it takes for most of the thoughts to move to the right side. Don't stress or strain about this, but just feel it as something natural occurring within your mind. These thoughts seem to belong on the right side for now, and you are just letting them migrate there at their own pace. Remain very relaxed.

Over on the left side, as the thoughts migrate away, there is a peaceful emptiness beginning to form. There may be a few stray thoughts still around, but the peace is clearly there. Now imagine a soft, comforting light filling the empty space, a light that emanates love from within the space. Imagine the center of who you are moves over into the peace, taking up residence within the light and peace and love. Focus all your attention in that peaceful place.

That light and peace and love is the Inner Spirit, your connection to God. Experiencing this place puts you in touch with the memory of your True Home. Once you find this place, you will have a new home you can go to whenever you need to get away from the crazy ego world of pain and guilt and fear. Simply feel this place for as long as you like. When you are done, take a couple of deep breaths, open your eyes and return to your everyday life. The Inner Spirit is here whenever you wish to find it.

Practice this meditation regularly and then when you practice forgiveness, you will be more able to find the Inner Spirit. You may discover this peaceful place, or you may experience the Inner Spirit as more of a spiritual personality you can talk to. In either case, what is important is that you find a place of peace where you can go when you are ready to forgive. The Inner Spirit knows the non-loving thoughts you are forgiving are all illusions, and these illusions will disappear as you remember where you came from.

Regular Practice

As you begin this practice you may find your connection to the Inner Spirit to be fleeting. It may seem like only a feeling or a brief image, and sometimes nothing may appear to be happening at all. This is normal. In time, you will find the Inner Spirit if you have a focused intent. In order to make the connection more consistent, you will need to commit to a regular practice, some time set aside on a regular schedule.

How you go about this is unique for each person based on what your everyday life is like. You do not need to retreat from life in order to find a few minutes a day or even every other day to quiet your mind. In some cultures, meditative practice is reserved for special settings and times. For us, we need only commit to finding a time and place where there are not too many distractions. This may be difficult, but it's certainly worth making a little effort.

It is also helpful to simply think about the Inner Spirit during the day even when you do not have enough time to seriously practice. This reinforces your bond to the Inner Spirit, and will help you in your everyday life. One way to do this is to put a reminder someplace where you will see it several times a day. This will help you stay centered during the day as the ego tries to turn your focus away from your inner life to all the distractions in the external world.

It also might be a good idea to acknowledge the Inner Spirit before you go to sleep at night. This sets up your focus as you enter the sleep state, which can influence your sleep and your dreams. Remember the Inner Spirit is there to help you any way it can, including improving your sleep and changing your dreams. This just gives you one more opportunity to touch the Inner Spirit.

As you follow a regular practice, you can expect the connection within your mind will grow. It may happen quickly or it may take some time, but it doesn't matter as long as you try consistently.

Finding the Inner Spirit

There is benefit in touching the Inner Spirit on a frequent basis even if you do none of the rest of the process of forgiveness. The Inner Spirit is a place of comfort and peace within a chaotic world, and the comfort will grow as you continue this practice.

You should find that your connection to the Inner Spirit increases your motivation to practice forgiveness in your life. By realizing there is a choice you can make away from the ego's vision of life, you will want to rid yourself of your non-loving thoughts. You will want to see the people around you in a new way, no longer separate, but connected to you just as you are connected to the Inner Spirit.

The Inner Spirit resides in every separated mind, and we all have the ability to touch that Spirit, and through this contact, to radically change how we see, feel, and think about everything in this world. Whether you believe it now or not, finding the Inner Spirit is the most inevitable thing in your life. It is only up to you to decide to start looking.

In the next chapter, you'll learn the full process of forgiveness, taking your list of non-loving thoughts and your new relationship with the Inner Spirit, and applying a three-step process to each of those non-loving thoughts, freeing them from your mind.

How to Practice Forgiveness

We've come a long way on our road to true forgiveness. We've seen how forgiveness is practiced in other cultures and religions. We've explored a new philosophy of Love and God, and learned how we've taken a wrong turn as we listen primarily to the ego. We've learned how to recognize our non-loving thoughts and begun to make a list of these thoughts to use for practicing forgiveness. We've learned the importance of the Inner Spirit, our connection to God, and how we can touch the inner part of ourselves. With these tools at hand, we are now ready to learn the process of forgiveness.

As we begin this next step, hopefully you will have started your list of non-loving thoughts, which you will use as the raw material for practicing forgiveness. If you haven't started a list, you may want to write down one or two non-loving thoughts now to use as we go through the process. You may want to take a moment or two to connect with your Inner Spirit in preparation as well, using whatever method you find works best for you. If you still feel the Inner Spirit eludes you, don't worry. It's all about repetition and intent. If you keep at it, success will come.

But before we look at the specifics of the technique, it's important to clear the air about other methods of forgiveness and why these do not work within our philosophy. We want to look at the fundamental flaws in the way forgiveness is practiced in other religions, philosophies, and psychologies. This should help you to focus specifically on this method as you reject the methods you may have learned in your life. Once we see what forgiveness is not, we will describe what forgiveness is.

What Forgiveness Is Not

We looked at forgiveness in other cultures in the first chapter, and discussed a common approach to forgiveness which is used in several religions and philosophies and often in modern psychology. In this approach, one first recognizes he has been the victim of an attack from another. This attack can be verbal, an emotional slight, or a physical attack. It doesn't matter what the form is, it only matters that one person feels he has been wronged.

Once someone feels wronged, the religion, philosophy, or psychology tells the person it's important for him to forgive whoever attacked him. In some religions, forgiveness is not required unless the party who wronged you asks for forgiveness. In others and in psychology, it's generally considered beneficial to forgive no matter what the other party does. In all cases, it is considered to be helpful to an individual to forgive others.

In some cases there is a clear series of steps this forgiveness should take, which might include a direct communication to the individual of the intention to forgive. If another person has asked for forgiveness, one should grant forgiveness willingly and not hold back. In a religious context, the forgiving person might also ask God to forgive the other person as well.

In the second form of this common forgiveness, someone may feel he has wronged another person and is seeking forgiveness for himself. This person is trying to absolve himself of the guilt he feels, and the act of seeking forgiveness begins the process. This might include apologizing to the other person, and perhaps offering some penance, monetary or otherwise. Again in a religious context, asking God for forgiveness may be a final step.

In some religions, one must ask the other individual for forgiveness for some attack you made on that person. You would only ask God for forgiveness for acts which were against God. In other religions, it matters not what you have done, it is possible to pray to God for forgiveness in all cases. In fact, it is sometimes recommended you pray for some kind of blanket forgiveness, since you may not even realize some of the sins you have committed.

From our point of view, the problem with all these approaches is the person believes a real attack has occurred, either from another or toward another. In order for one to even consider forgiveness, the attack, even if only verbal or mental, must be seen as real and must be seen to have an effect on another. The guilt that is felt is real and the absolution of the guilt must occur through this process.

One looks to the external to absolve the guilt that is felt. The forgiveness requires some degree of focus on the external world in order to work. In some cases, forgiving another requires you to communicate with the person, but even if it doesn't, it still requires that you look squarely in the world for where the attack originally occurred. And if one tries to seek forgiveness from God, it is from a God that is outside us, one that can forgive, but one that can also judge us.

We are trying to see things a different way. In our philosophy, all such attacks are illusions and therefore not real. If the person sees them as real, true forgiveness cannot occur. We are promised that at our core, we are all without guilt, and if this is true, we and the others around us do not need to be forgiven for the attacks we make on each other, because those attacks are illusory.

The only conclusion is that this common form of forgiveness is another ploy of the ego, another way to keep you trapped in the idea of separation. The attack, if it is seen as real, increases the separation you feel between yourself and another person. Because you have followed the tenets of your religion or philosophy or therapist, you might feel you are further on the path to being a better person, but this is a meaningless exercise.

This false forgiveness includes asking God to forgive you or another person. In our philosophy, God knows what you think you see as an attack never really happened – it's just an illusion. God as Pure Love can never see anything you do as wrong, and can never judge you guilty. You are now and always will be perfect in God's eyes. What would God need to forgive you for?

Once again this attempt to ask God for forgiveness is just another tool of the ego, reinforcing the belief you are guilty. Only by eliminating guilt will you begin to free yourself from the hold of the ego, and the way to eliminate the guilt is by learning the true method of forgiveness. In the next section we will discover how true forgiveness works, but it is important to realize you need to throw out your old concept of forgiveness in order to see a new way.

What Forgiveness Is

If we are going to throw out these old ideas of forgiveness, we need to find a new kind of forgiveness to take its place. This new approach to forgiveness is radically different from what we have been taught in this world, but it has the potential to fundamentally change your life and all your interactions with the world around you.

We will present a definition of forgiveness in the context of our philosophy, and throughout the rest of the book, will learn ways to apply this forgiveness in a practical way. We define forgiveness in three ways – one each for past, present, and future:

Forgiveness is realizing the illusion you believed in never happened.

Forgiveness is realizing the illusion you believe in does not exist.

Forgiveness is realizing the illusion you fear will not occur.

Now let's break these definitions apart to better understand what is going on. First we see the word 'realizing' which means forgiveness is a process of understanding and therefore purely a process of the mind. Forgiveness does not require any external action whatsoever and believing such action is required will negate the whole process.

The second word of note is 'illusion' and once again this is in the mind. In a moment we will look more closely at all the different kinds of illusions one might forgive, but for now we will use the simple definition – an illusion is any non-loving thought. It is these non-loving thoughts we are forgiving, whether they are about the external world we believe we live in or about ourselves.

Next the definition points out that these illusions are simply something you believe in or fear, again purely of the mind. The ego presents a picture of the world and we believe in that vision and we fear what the future of this world may be. The ego tells you there are rules you need to live by, and though you believe these rules come from the world around you, they are only beliefs, the beliefs of your illusory ego self. These rules and beliefs form the basis for this world and the basis for all the guilt and fear and pain in this world.

And finally the crux of forgiveness is that these illusions never happened, do not exist, and will not occur. It is in this moment of realization you can free yourself from the ego view of the world and instead touch your true place of connection with the Inner Spirit. When your non-loving thoughts are seen as illusions, then the forgiveness is complete, and the illusion will be gone, leaving peace in its place. As you continue this way of forgiveness, your beliefs about the world will change.

Now you see why it is so important to begin to recognize your non-loving thoughts. These are the illusions the ego wants us to believe are real. This is why we create the list, so we can focus on each of these thoughts, and through this process of forgiveness, let them free. If there is strong emotion attached to a thought you are forgiving and you apply forgiveness completely with the help of the Inner Spirit, the heavy emotions will fade and you will feel lighter.

You can also see why it is imperative we connect with the Inner Spirit in order to achieve this forgiveness. If we try to forgive while being our everyday ego self, the ego will find ways to convince you that you have achieved something you haven't. This is what the ego is really good at – deceiving us into believing we are doing something important and loving, when we are just going through the motions.

If we make the connection to the Inner Spirit and experience the place of unconditional love and peace, the ego will be thwarted. The one place in the mind where the ego cannot survive is in a truly loving space, and all the illusions the ego presents us will disappear within this space as well. When we choose the Inner Spirit as our guide, we will touch our True Self within the Mind of God. Only loving thoughts will remain.

This is the promise of forgiveness. All of your thoughts will be loving ones, and you will see all of those around you as perfect, free of any guilt. Within this place of love you will experience peace within a world you only saw as chaotic before. By practicing forgiveness regularly, you can reach this place. It may take time and there may be setbacks, but if your intent is true and your non-loving thoughts fall away one by one, the outcome is assured.

Now that we have a definition for forgiveness, it's time to learn how to forgive. What will be presented here is a simple three-step process which can be applied over and over to every non-loving thought you wish to forgive. It is the repeatability and simplicity of this method that makes it powerful.

You may find due to your beliefs or past meditation practices that you want to modify this procedure in some ways to something which is more comfortable for you. This is fine as long as the essence of the three steps is achieved – you choose a non-loving thought, you connect with the inner part of yourself which connects you to God, and you realize the thought you had with all the attendant emotions is an illusion. The exact form is not important, but the essence is.

The Process of Forgiveness

So we are ready to forgive. We have taken the time to begin a list of non-loving thoughts. We have put aside some time each day to connect with the Inner Spirit, so when we're ready to forgive, we can touch that place in our minds at will and know any resistance we feel will be overcome. These two simple steps are the basis for the final step of forgiveness.

Step 1 – Identifying a Non-Loving Thought

We learned in the third chapter how to start a list of our non-loving thoughts. By now you should have at least several items on this list, and maybe many items, depending on how diligently you worked on it. It's now time to start working with the list and to discover how these unhappy, non-loving thoughts can be freed from your mind through this process of forgiveness.

You should continue to add new entries to your list, even after you have started to forgive some of the items. There should be no shortage of non-loving thoughts to be found in the mind, the mind which is ruled too often by the ego. We want to continue to grow the list, for this is a recognition that so many of your thoughts about the world are non-loving. In time, as you have success at forgiving, there may be fewer items to add, but for now finding new things to forgive should not be a problem.

So the first step in the process will be to select an item from the list. This sounds like a simple task, but since there is emotion associated with these non-loving thoughts, we need to be sure that bias doesn't enter into the choice. Here are some ways to avoid this bias.

Count down the list 5 or 6 items and select that one. The next time you choose, count from that item 5 or 6 further down, and continue this way each time you choose. If you reach the end, go back to the beginning and count down 3 or 4 items and continue.

Hold the list in front of you and close your eyes and point to an item on the list. If this is one you have already forgiven, do it again until you hit one you haven't yet forgiven.

Start from the end of the list and work forward for several items, then go back to the beginning and choose the next several items, then back to the next one at the bottom, etc.

One of these methods should work for you and allow you to choose items in a fairly random order. The most important thing is not to reject an item because you think it's too difficult or too trivial or for any other reason. From the point of view of the Inner Spirit, every non-loving thought is a barrier to love, so we must be open to forgiving all the non-loving thoughts we find in our minds. Now that we have chosen an item we will take a few moments to connect with the Inner Spirit.

Step 2 – Connecting with the Inner Spirit

We looked at the concept of the Inner Spirit in the fourth chapter. There we learned that the Inner Spirit is the part of the separated self that remembers the Mind of God. As we stated, there is nothing unique about the name Inner Spirit, and if you prefer to call it something else, that is fine. Names are not important to this philosophy.

What is important is that this part of us, this place within our minds, is the connection between the separated world we believe in and the Home within the Mind of God our True Self has never left. Since we believe so thoroughly in all the illusions the ego has presented to us, we need help in finding our way to forgiveness. The Inner Spirit is our communication link between the illusory world of the ego and the real world of God.

The Inner Spirit offers us a bridge back to our True Home, and through this bridge, we will be able to release all of our illusions. The Inner Spirit, being true to God, is never judgmental about these illusions. Whatever illusion you bring, whether seemingly minor or horrendous, will instantly disappear. Because the ego will always try to prevent us from realizing true forgiveness, we need to be able to access the Inner Spirit within our minds in order to forgive.

In the previous chapter, you learned a technique for quieting your mind and getting in touch with your Inner Spirit. By now you should have tried to touch this loving quiet place in your mind, and have begun to set aside time each day to do this. This gives you the opportunity to turn off the constant ego thoughts which keep your world spinning, to be away from the noise and clamor of normal life, and find the still place within. This connection to the Inner Spirit is a critical part of forgiveness, and making the connection should be a lifelong commitment.

Now as the next step in the process of forgiveness, sit in your quiet place and relax and breathe easily and say to yourself, "I want to touch the Inner Spirit within my mind." Repeat it slowly and as you do, look around within your mind for the place that feels most peaceful. When you find that place, turn your attention there and continue to repeat the phrase. Feel the connection as fully as you can. Feel the love and peace you find in the space. Absorb everything the Inner Spirit offers you.

Once you've made this connection, you now have everything you need to proceed to the actual forgiveness – a non-loving thought you want to forgive and a full experience of the Inner Spirit, who will help you through the process.

Step 3 – Forgiving the Experience

So let's try an example. Take the non-loving thought you chose with the feelings of fear, anger, guilt, etc. associated with it. Bring the thought to the front of your mind, focus on it intently. Feel all the emotions surrounding it, immersing yourself in the full experience of the event. If possible, imagine those emotions as something physical, like a dark, roiling ball of ugliness.

It's critical that you let yourself feel the emotions fully – the guilt, fear, pain, hate, grief, anger – and not hold back. All of the emotions surrounding the non-loving thought are the result of your focus on the ego's way of viewing the world through the lens of separation. You must be willing to look clearly at this non-loving thought in order to attain true forgiveness. Let the emotions flow, see the events in clear detail, knowing the Inner Spirit will replace all of this pain with love.

Holding that focus, begin to forgive everything associated with this experience. We have learned that all these feelings and thoughts are illusions presented to us by our egos. You will focus on the people involved in the event as the first part of your forgiveness. So forgive each person with any connection to these thoughts, saying "I forgive..." followed by the person's name, repeating it several times. Visualize the individual involved and see them face to face as you repeat the words of forgiveness.

Then forgive the experience itself, for the entire experience associated with this non-loving thought was an illusion created by the ego. The Inner Spirit recognizes the illusion and stands ready to help you free it. See the experience in all its detail, reliving every aspect of it as you now say, "I forgive..." followed by what you call the event, and then "... knowing this is just an illusion created by the ego."

Next take that roiling ball of ugliness, with all the emotions tied into this experience, with all the images of the people involved, and with all the detail of the event, and hand it off to the Inner Spirit, who remembers the Mind of God and knows these emotions and thoughts are illusions with no power whatsoever. This releases the experience, the emotions, and the non-loving false thoughts. The ego loses some of its hold on you as your awareness of the Inner Spirit reminds you of where you belong.

As one final step, say "I forgive myself", for it was you, as your ego self, who had all these thoughts and emotions originally. By forgiving yourself you release yourself from the heavy weight of responsibility for this negative experience, and because of this, you will naturally feel closer to the Inner Spirit. Now take a moment to just sit with the Inner Spirit and thank the Inner Spirit for its help. This moment of connection will solidify the act of forgiveness.

You should take a moment to observe how you are feeling. If the process has been followed and you felt the connection to the Inner Spirit, you should feel a sense of peace and comfort where before you may have been in a more negative state. Forgiveness changes who you are and how you feel. The emotions which have been dragging you down in your life can be lifted away through this process, leaving you feeling more empowered and confident.

These are real changes we are talking about. The ego has been your close companion for your whole life, and now you are reversing course, letting the Inner Spirit be your guide instead. Continuing to forgive the next non-loving thought and the next will alter how you see the world around you, and ultimately this will lead you back to your True Home.

You should now move on to another non-loving thought, following the same procedure as before. Choose another random item from your list, perhaps this time finding something further back in time or a fear about the future. It doesn't matter how important or trivial the thought might seem, the process is the same no matter when the thought and associated emotions first occurred. If it's a non-loving thought, it's still an illusion and the Inner Spirit stands ready to release you from it.

Once you are done forgiving a non-loving thought, don't delete the item from your list. Just make a mark or note by the item on the list. This will show your progress on the path to forgiveness. After you have done this for awhile, you will have many marks by the items on your list. When you reread those marked items, you should have an entirely different emotional reaction toward them. If you have truly forgiven in the way we just discussed, the attachment you had to those items will have melted away. It is through this accumulation of marked items that your emotional freedom will grow.

As you continue to add new items to the list, and you practice forgiveness and mark items off, you may find that items you haven't yet forgiven which were strongly emotional for you, may no longer hold such attachment. Once you start forgiveness for some items, the forgiveness will naturally spread to others without making conscious effort. The Inner Spirit can continue to work in the background, and the fact you are giving this process your attention increases the forgiveness in your life.

To review the process, begin by selecting a non-loving thought to forgive. Take a moment to touch the place within where you can find the Inner Spirit, your connection to God. Then say "I forgive..." followed first by the names of everyone involved, then followed by a description of the illusory event, and once more followed by "myself." Pass all the negative emotions associated with the non-loving thought to the Inner Spirit to be released. Finally mark the item on your list as one you have forgiven.

Developing a Regular Practice

Now you're ready to begin a regular practice. Forgiving a few of the non-loving thoughts in your mind will get you started on the path, but true forgiveness will be a lifelong learning process. Without regular practice, the ego will maintain its control over your everyday life. Without practice, non-loving thoughts will influence every aspect of your experience. You must commit to a practice if you want to end your perception of pain, guilt, fear, and death in your life and in the world around you.

If at this moment in your life, you decide you want something better, something more loving and kind and peaceful, you will have all the help you will need. The Inner Spirit is with you always, and as you practice, will alter your experience of the world. You will see people differently, no longer bound by your negative impressions. You will experience new events, ones driven by feelings of love and compassion. All this help is yours and all these changes are possible once you commit to the practice.

So set aside a brief time every day to forgive a few of your non-loving thoughts. Make this commitment to a small bit of time your number one priority. After awhile, you can increase this process to several times a day as it becomes more and more natural. Eventually you may find yourself doing it without having to think about it too seriously. Once this daily practice becomes second nature, you can begin to apply the technique in real time to events in your life.

You will experience resistance along the way, for the ego will not let go easily. It's important you maintain your intent and focus in order to overcome the obstacles placed in your way. You must put forgiveness into practice, applying it to all the events of your life, if you want to free yourself from the ego's hold. Remember the Inner Spirit is connected to who you really are, and ultimately the ego's world is destined to fade away.

The ultimate goal is for you to realize when non-loving thoughts occur and to instantly forgive them. This can lead to a state of continual forgiveness, a state where every unpleasant experience in your life is immediately turned around through forgiveness. Think about it. All the fear, pain, anger, sadness, and guilt you've felt over the years being instantly forgiven. This state of continual forgiveness will lead to the state of Peace, for if all your non-loving thoughts are being forgiven, the ego has lost its hold on you, and all that will be left is Love.

You have now learned the process of forgiveness. You have made a list of your non-loving thoughts. You have begun to take some quiet time each day to connect with the Inner Spirit. You have followed the three-step procedure to forgive some of these non-loving thoughts. Hopefully as you see the results of forgiveness in your life, you will be more motivated to continue the practice. You will begin to see more unconditional love and peace in your life. This is our goal and it is a realistic, achievable goal. It will be your intent and willingness which will determine your success.

In order to help you in this process, in the next chapter we will examine many examples of forgiveness, sorted by categories. This can serve as a reference when you need to understand better how to apply forgiveness in the future. In the following chapter, we will learn about continual forgiveness and how to transition from a regular practice to the instantaneous application of forgiveness.

Applying the Practice

Now that we've explored the process of forgiveness, we are going to look at several examples of ways to apply forgiveness. We'll explore examples of projecting non-loving thoughts out into the world and perceiving non-loving thoughts coming at us. We'll see instances of directing non-loving thoughts at oneself, potentially leading to feelings of guilt and depression. As we focus on the different kinds of non-loving thoughts, we'll discover how the three-step process of forgiveness can free us from the negative feelings and experiences in our lives.

Throughout these examples, we're going to look at the non-loving thoughts of two fictional characters, Sarah and Jason. We'll discover these two have a wide range of issues as we focus on their lives, but the hope is that you will see some of your own issues and non-loving thoughts in these examples. The reality is as long as we inhabit this physical world, we will all have some of these thoughts, and it's best if we look them squarely in the eye and face up to what's going on in our minds.

In each of these examples, imagine you are friends with Sarah and Jason and they are telling you about something that's happened or a fear of something happening in the future. Each example will start with a conversational snippet from one of them. This will be followed by the item added to the list of non-loving thoughts. After a brief discussion of the situation, the process of forgiveness will be applied to the item. At the end will be some comments about the possible outcome. We'll look at the emotional responses Sarah or Jason have to a particular event, seeing how non-loving these responses are, and how these can change through forgiveness.

Examples of Anger

Example 1:

> Sarah: "I've really had it with Sheila. She was over here calling me a loser again today, and I told her off, and called her a b*%#*! She's not going to treat me that way anymore!"

> "I am so angry with Sheila for calling me a loser."

Sarah and Sheila are sisters and have had a love/hate relationship throughout their lives. Growing up together, Sheila always seemed to be the favorite in the family, and as they got older, she was the one with the great career and good relationships. Sarah struggled financially and in relating to others, and she felt Sheila never let her forget her problems. This led to resentment on both their parts, and ultimately to many angry outbursts.

Sarah has decided it's time to heal her relationship with Sheila. She wants to forgive her, and through learning this new technique of forgiveness, she has begun to make a list of her non-loving thoughts. She has also begun to meditate and feels like she has found some connection to the Inner Spirit. She chooses the non-loving thought about her anger with Sheila, and goes to her quiet place inside.

Sarah feels all the years of anger and even hatred she feels toward Sheila. She lets all the terrible negative emotion sweep through her to the point where she can barely control herself. At the same time she concentrates as best she can on the place in her mind where she can feel the peace of the Inner Spirit. She repeats over and over, "I forgive Sheila and I forgive all the awful times we've had together for I know these were just illusions from the ego." Then, "I forgive myself for expressing so much anger." She continues repeating the phrases, until she finally hands all this pain and anger and hatred to the Inner Spirit to be released.

As Sarah experiences the quiet place inside, she feels something changing in her. She visualizes Sheila and in place of all the anger and hatred, she remembers some of the good times together, some of the love they have shared. She thanks the Inner Spirit for helping her see the whole situation in a new light, and as a final step, she checks the item off her list, knowing true forgiveness has occurred.

Example 2:

> Jason: "The other morning I had to take my son to school and got caught in traffic. I was about an hour late for work, and we had an important meeting planned first thing. After the meeting, my boss, Jim, really laid into me. He yelled and called me all kinds of names. I felt really bad about being late, but I couldn't believe how out of control Jim was. He had no right to say some of those things to me. He's such a jerk!"
>
> "Jim got really angry with me for being late."

Jason has a wife and three kids, and these family responsibilities require a great deal of his time and energy. He's pretty good at balancing it all with his work, but sometimes his home life interferes with his work life. On this day, Jim wasn't interested in any excuses and became extremely angry with him. Jason's tardiness had impacted others in the office and that was unacceptable. Jason felt guilty about it, but also felt Jim was way out of line with his behavior. His first reaction was to get angry back at Jim, but he didn't think it would help.

One evening several days later, when the kids were all in bed, Jason took a few moments to try to forgive Jim for what happened. He found a quiet spot and went into a deeply relaxed state, using a meditation technique he'd learned years ago. He touched the place in his mind where he felt the peace and love of the Inner Spirit.

He remembered all the minute details of his encounter with Jim, everything Jim said to him and all the emotions he felt as Jim yelled at him. At first he felt guilt for letting everyone down, but as Jim became more and more angry, he felt anger as well, knowing he was being unjustly accused. The guilt and anger welled up in him, as he tried to hold his focus on the Inner Spirit. He repeated several times, "I forgive Jim for all his anger and I forgive the whole experience, knowing this was a creation of the ego." He then said, "I forgive myself for reacting with guilt and anger, instead of love."

He then passed all the negative emotions off to the Inner Spirit, freeing them from his mind. As he did, he felt lighter, less stressed and upset. What had seemed like an overwhelmingly ugly experience could now be seen as just another ego illusion. He even felt a sense of love for Jim which emanated from the Inner Spirit. Finally he checked this item off his list and went to bed in a peaceful place.

Examples of Fear

Example 3:

> Jason: "I heard about the burglary down the street last week. The owners were in the house and managed to scare the burglars away. I really worry about that happening to us. If something happened to the kids, I don't know if I could deal with it. It's so scary sometimes."

> "I'm scared about a criminal doing something to the kids."

Jason's family is the most important thing in his life. He does everything he can to put his wife and kids first. This means trying to balance a busy, stressful work life with all the commitments he makes at home. But along with these responsibilities, he worries that something out of his control could happen to his family. Like so many people, he hears about terrible crimes and believes he and his family could just as easily fall victim to a random crime.

As Jason tries to learn this new way of forgiveness, he realizes these thoughts of fear are another non-loving thought, one he adds to his list. Now when he has a few quiet moments one day at lunch, he chooses this thought to forgive. He closes his office door, turns off his phone, and sits quietly for a few moments, trying his best to touch the peaceful place in his mind, the place of the Inner Spirit. Once he relaxes and feels this peacefulness, he proceeds to forgive.

He first imagines all the awful crimes that could befall his family. This is extremely painful to him, thinking about what might happen. But he knows he has to feel this pain and fear in order to forgive the non-loving thought. As he holds his focus on this fear and at the same time on the Inner Spirit, he says, "I forgive all the imagined crimes that might happen to me and my family in the future, knowing it is my ego that creates these thoughts in my mind." Then, "I forgive myself for all these fearful thoughts."

He takes all the pain and fear and passes it to the peaceful place in his mind, where the Inner Spirit is waiting to release it. Though he knows some of these fearful thoughts might resurface in the future, for now he feels a weight lifted away, and he realizes he can love his family more completely if he doesn't worry about the future all the time. With that, he checks the item off his list.

Example 4:

Sarah: "You know, my aunt died last month and ever since I can't stop thinking about dying. I feel like I believe in

God, but nobody seems to really know what happens when you die. Sometimes I feel terrified at the thought of dying."

"I'm really scared of what will happen when I die."

Since she was a little girl, Sarah has been afraid of death. When she was eight, her grandmother died and Sarah had to look at her in the casket, an image she's never forgotten. She had nightmares for months after that. As she got older, she began to understand death more as a part of life, but the fundamental fear never went away. When she thought about her own death, it was always a scary thing. She couldn't seem to separate who she was from her body, so the thought of being put in the ground or being cremated was very painful and personal for her. Believing in a God and that some kind of afterlife might exist was not enough to ease the fear associated with her body.

So today Sarah chooses this as her next non-loving thought to forgive. She finds a few moments to touch her Inner Spirit, the place of love and peace and fearlessness inside her. She then begins by remembering the scene with her grandmother's body and all the fear she felt. She imagines her body being buried or burned up after she's dead and feels that fear and pain. She immerses herself in these horrid images to the point where she can barely stand it.

Now she says, "I forgive all my experiences of death in this world, including my fears about my own death, knowing death is only an illusion created by my ego, an illusion with no reality." She repeats it over and over, until it's truth begins to sink in. Then she says, "I forgive myself for using death as a way to separate myself from God." With this she hands all this fear of death, this fear of an illusion, to the Inner Spirit, allowing the fear to disappear, and in its place she experiences for a brief moment the timelessness and eternal life that is God. She sits quietly in this place, basking in this peace, and then when she's done she puts a check next to this item on her list.

Examples of Guilt

Example 5:

> Sarah: "I was watching TV and saw the guy who molested those children. He looked so slimy. There's no question he's guilty and I hope he gets what's coming to him."
>
> "I saw a child molester on TV and I know he's guilty."

We all learn at an early age from our parents, our schools, our religions, and from the media, that there is crime and eventual punishment in the world. We learn about our 'justice' system, which is supposed to seek out the crimes in the world and punish the offenders and support the victims. Sarah has learned all of this and she's certain she can recognize a guilty person when she sees one. In this case she learns of someone accused of child molestation, one of the most heinous crimes Sarah knows of. Just by looking at him, she is certain of his guilt

Today she chooses this non-loving thought from her list and initially cringes. She doesn't really want to think she can forgive such a person, but she knows she is not supposed to reject anything on her list. She knows she will certainly need the help of the Inner Spirit for this one, so she goes to her quiet place and before she thinks about the guilty person, she finds the place of love and tranquility in her mind. She fully embraces that place, letting the peace wash over her.

Trying to hold that focus, she thinks about the child molester. She lets herself imagine the experience of the child, the victim. She feels the fear and pain and shame the child felt, and she sees the offender and feels all the anger she has for him. She then says repeatedly, "I forgive this whole situation, because the terrible things we believe we see in this world are ultimately illusions and not of God. I forgive the perpetrator for his illusory act and the child for its illusory fear and pain. The Loving God would never let such a reality exist." Finally, "I forgive myself, as my ego self, for projecting this guilt and then perceiving it in the world."

When she finishes, she passes all these images and feelings off to the Inner Spirit to vanish from her mind. As she now thinks about the whole experience, she realizes it was her strong attraction to this event which made it seem so real to her. She now feels the attraction fading, to be replaced by simple love for everyone involved. With this new understanding, she checks this item off.

Example 6:

> Jason: "I'm so upset today. Our next door neighbors' boy, Andy, was riding his bike on the street and I was heading out for work in the car and got distracted and hit him. I think he's got a broken arm. I can't believe how stupid I was."

> "I hit Andy on his bike and broke his arm because I was hurrying and not paying attention."

Jason loves his kids and would never want to see anyone hurt them in any way. So when he hit Andy on his bike, simply because he was rushing to work, he felt terrible. He felt ashamed and didn't want to tell anybody about it, even though he knew everyone in the neighborhood would find out. In spite of all he did for his own kids, in this case he was really careless about someone else's child. He felt like a bad person, and he wondered if he could ever get over the guilt. But as Jason was learning, guilt is ultimately another of the ego's tools for keeping us from experiencing love. As long as he was focused on his guilt, he would be unable to fully express love to others and to accept love in his life.

He chose this non-loving thought one evening as he sat down for one of his regular forgiveness sessions. He began as always with some quiet time to touch his Inner Spirit. He had begun to envision the Inner Spirit in the form of a great person, one who expressed only love and comfort. He basked in the feelings of this love and as he did, he entered a deep peaceful place. Now he began to relive the experience of leaving for work that morning, hitting Andy on his bike, seeing him in pain, and eventually watching as the ambulance took him away. He felt all the sadness and guilt he felt that day.

At the same time he touched his Inner Spirit, and with this peaceful focus, he then said repeatedly, "I forgive the experience of hitting Andy and breaking his arm, because I know this non-loving thought is an illusion from the ego." Next he said, "I forgive myself for my feelings of guilt and sadness and anger at myself for these were creations of the ego." This he repeated over and over, and as he did he passed all these non-loving thoughts and feelings to the Inner Spirit, knowing they would be released.

Once he was through, he felt the weight of guilt lifting from him. He realized as long as he was concentrating on feeling guilty, he couldn't express love in his life. He now felt the love welling up inside him, a love for Andy and his own family and a general love for all who shared the world with him. Forgiveness freed him to see those around him in a new light, a light with no guilt attached. Finally he checked this one off the list.

Examples of Conditional Love

Example 7:

Jason: "My Mom just drives me crazy sometimes. I really love her, but I wish she wouldn't be so judgmental all the

time. She's always correcting me about the way we're rais-
ing the kids, as if she was the greatest Mom ever. I want
her in my life, but I want her to back off."

"I love Mom, but she drives me crazy with all her criti-
cism."

For most of us, our relationships with our parents are some of
the closest throughout our lives, but are also often ones of ongo-
ing conflict. Jason grew up in a conventional family and has always loved his mother, but has at times felt smothered by her. As
a child, he felt she was overly critical and over-protective toward
him. This has continued into adulthood, and now that he has
children, he wants them to have a relationship with their grandmother, but he finds it hard to be around her. Her constant criti-
cism is making him angry.

Jason's relationship with his mother is clearly one of conditional
love. He feels he would love her better if she would only behave
differently. Realizing this, he adds this non-loving thought to his
list. When he next chooses this item, he first connects with the
Inner Spirit. He then begins to remember the multitude of experiences he's had with his mother, focusing especially on situations in which he felt criticized. He feels deeply how that crit-
icism has influenced his beliefs about himself. He realizes how it
has affected his relationships throughout his life.

So he begins, "I forgive Mom for everything she's done that I
thought was hurting me. I forgive all those times I felt Mom was
criticizing me knowing these were illusions the ego used to increase our separation." He repeats it and then says, "I forgive
myself for not loving Mom unconditionally, for wanting her to be
different so I could love her more." He takes all those feelings of
low self-worth and all the anger he'd felt toward his mother and
passes these to the Inner Spirit to completely disappear.

With this new emotional freedom, he can now see his mother differently, as just another self on the same journey he is on to find a way Home. He truly feels he can love her unconditionally. When she tries to criticize him now, he responds with only love and as he does, his perception of her is fundamentally changed. With this new way of seeing, he is ready to check this item off the list.

Example 8:

> Sarah: "I remember when I was 25 and I fell in love with Michael. It was so wonderful. I thought about him every minute of the day. He seemed to love me just as much, calling me all the time. I knew we were going to be together forever. But eventually we drifted apart and he started dating someone else. I just wish I could go back to that time."

> "I was so in love with Michael and it all fell apart. I wish I could relive those times."

One of the most common forms of conditional love is an infatuation with another person. This feeling of being 'in love' is one of the most powerful, intense emotions we can feel in life. As part of this, the object of our love is seen in ideal terms, as someone with no or a minimum of flaws, and most importantly as someone who has the same feelings of love for us. Sarah threw herself completely into the relationship with Michael, believing this was what love was all about and believing it could last forever.

Over time, things changed, and what had begun as a seemingly perfect relationship was seen to have cracks in it. Little things began to irritate both of them, and eventually what had seemed so perfect was becoming more and more difficult. Finally separation was the only answer. Sarah chose this experience as her non-loving thought to forgive one evening. She began with her meditation which put her in touch with the peaceful place of the Inner Spirit.

Then she began to feel all the emotions of the experience, the joy of the infatuation, the little problems along the way, and finally the awful pain and heartbreak of the separation. It was almost too much to bear, feeling these two extremes, but she held her focus on it, knowing the Inner Spirit and forgiveness would help. She said, "I forgive Michael for simply being himself. I forgive my whole relationship with Michael, both good and bad, knowing the extreme pleasure and extreme pain were both from the ego." Then, "I forgive myself for not loving Michael unconditionally and for expressing so much anger and hurt."

She took all this pain and sadness and passed this to the Inner Spirit. She now tried to focus on the real Michael, just another individual on the journey. She can love him unconditionally just as she can with anyone whenever she is in touch with the truth, love, and peace of the Inner Spirit. She now can see potential new relationships in a new light, as she sees the difference between love and being 'in love'. This item gets checked off the list.

Examples of Grief

Example 9:

Sarah: "When Michael and I broke up, I went into mourning. I was sad all the time and I couldn't do my work very well. It was such a big loss to me, it took me a year or more to get my life back to some kind of normal."

"I was grieving over the loss of my relationship with Michael."

Grief is most often associated with death and dying, but we can feel grief over any kind of loss, such as loss of a job, or loss of a relationship. Sarah was really distressed about the breakup with

Michael. She had put her heart and soul into the relationship, seeing a long future for the two of them. As it started to fall apart, she was upset, but kept believing something would happen to make it all right again. When the end finally came, she was devastated. All of her dreams about her life seemed to be shattered. She went into a state of mourning, as if someone close to her had died, but in this case it was her dream that died.

When she chose this non-loving thought of grief, she wasn't sure she could really forgive the situation entirely. But she knew through her previous successes at forgiving difficult thoughts that with the Inner Spirit's help, anything is possible. She found the quiet place inside and touched the peacefulness of the Inner Spirit. She focused on the feeling of loss and grief she'd experienced after the breakup. She saw the self she was then crying all the time, unable to function in a normal way. She immersed herself in those feelings of sadness.

She then said, "I forgive the whole experience after the breakup, knowing these feelings of loss and sadness were the result of the unrealistic expectations from my ego self." And, "I forgive myself for listening to the ego's outrageous dreams, and for not realizing I was creating my own sadness." Next she took all the grief, sadness, and feelings of loss, and handed these to the waiting Inner Spirit. These feelings were from the ego, an attempt to focus away from love and onto the death of the relationship.

Now Sarah felt a new freedom, a freedom from grief, knowing that love only brings grief and pain when she listens to the ego's ridiculous ideas of what love should be. True love is unconditional love and relationships based on unconditional love cannot result in pain. She believed she would not have to experience grief again when a relationship changed in some way. She could now happily check this item off the list.

Example 10:

> Jason: "I remember when Dad died. At first I couldn't believe it. He was such a strong man, but his heart just gave out. He was always someone I could go to if I needed help or guidance. I still miss having him in my life."
>
> "I'm still grieving over my Dad's death."

Grief is all about loss, and there seems to be no greater loss in our lives than death. From an early age we learn about death, whether it affects us personally or not. When it's personal, there is always a sense of loss. What was before a lively, animated human being is now just a lifeless shell. It sometimes seems strange and meaningless. Our religions tell us this person has gone to a better place, but no one can show us this place directly.

In our philosophy, death is just another illusory tool of the ego. The animated body that seemed to exist before was an illusion and the lifeless body that is left is an illusion. Jason has read and understands the philosophy, but his father was very real to him, and no matter what he understands intellectually, the loss of his father seems very real. He feels the grief of the loss, and it impacts how he lives his life.

Nevertheless, this is the item he selects one night and he's willing to forgive this non-loving thought if he can. He goes to the place where he feels connected to the Inner Spirit, knowing that place is what's real. He experiences the peace and love he finds there, where he is close to God, a God who knows that death is an illusion. He says, "I forgive the whole experience of Dad's death, and I forgive all the sadness and grief everyone felt for him, for I know these are only the ego's illusions." Then, "I forgive myself for being attracted to grief and loss and holding onto it for so long."

Jason takes all the feelings he has about losing his father, all the pain and sadness and grief, and hands these off to the loving presence of the Inner Spirit. In that space of peace and love, these sad feelings cannot exist. The True Self that was his father still lives in the Mind of God, and Jason must only get in touch with his connection to God, the Inner Spirit, to know we are all eternal and can never die. Feeling a sense of relief and comfort, he marks this item off the list.

Examples of Depression

Example 11:

> Jason: "When Billy was born and we found out he wasn't normal and would need years of care, I was so upset and depressed. You never think something like this could happen to you. I was angry with everybody and everything and just couldn't see any positive future."

> "I was depressed and angry when Billy was born."

Jason and his wife, Amy, had two kids and were looking forward to the birth of their third. The previous two births had been problem-free, so their expectations were for another simple birth. But immediately after Billy was born, problems with his heart were discovered. Extraordinary measures were required to keep him alive and he was in the hospital for several weeks. Jason and Amy were devastated. Jason felt overwhelmed trying to keep up with his work commitments and with his other kids during this time, in addition to offering support for Amy.

When they realized Billy's problems might be lifelong with multiple surgeries required, it was almost too much for them. They didn't know how they would manage all of this with everything else in life. Jason eventually fell into a deep depression, unable to see a happy future for his family. He couldn't give Amy and the other kids the support they needed, and his work suffered as well. He began to drink more in the evenings to dull the pain and pressure he felt, wanting to get away from the whole situation, but not seeing any way to do it.

Though Jason is now in a better place, when he looks back on that time, the feelings of depression and hopelessness are still very real to him. So tonight he chooses the non-loving thought of his depression as the item he wants to forgive. He gets in touch with his Inner Spirit and as he begins to feel all the raw emotion from that time, he says, "I forgive the whole experience of Billy's birth and the aftermath. I forgive my family and my job which I believed were dragging me down. I know all these perceptions and feelings were illusions from the ego." Then "I forgive myself for choosing depression as a way to deal with this situation."

He hands all the pain and fear and depression from that time off to the Inner Spirit to be released and healed. What is left is the powerful bond which was formed with his family during this time. He remembers just the happy and good moments, the loving moments. He now sees how this difficult experience brought his family together, and with that realization, he feels he can love them more fully. The item is checked off the list.

Example 12:

> Sarah: "Every time I see Sheila, she tells me I'm such a loser. The problem is I really believe her. Sometimes I feel I can't do anything right, and it's better if I just stay away from people. I go curl up in bed and try to forget everything."
>
> "I don't feel I'm worth a lot. I'm feeling depressed and useless."

Sarah's relationship with her sister, Sheila, has been fraught with conflict since they were little girls. In Sarah's eyes, Sheila seemed to do everything right, getting attention from the boys, making good grades, and eventually going on to college and a good career. Sarah struggled through school and could never have the social life she wanted. She had some friends, but they were the outcasts, and Sheila would always point this out to her.

As Sarah got older, these feelings of being less than others led to deeper feelings of poor self-worth, and ultimately to depression at times. When she was depressed, nothing in the world was worthwhile, not her job, her friends, or the simple pleasures of life. She would overeat and become sluggish and uninterested in getting out of the house. Now as she was beginning to practice forgiveness in her life, this day she chose her depression as the non-loving thought to forgive.

She knew she would really need the help of the Inner Spirit for this one, since during the times she was depressed, she always felt cut off from her inner life, unable to find the peace and love in her mind. Today she found that place, and as she settled there, she began to feel the low self-worth and the depression which had shaped much of her life. She thought about Sheila and how she would reinforce Sarah's low opinions of herself. She thought of those days she would shut out the world and stay in bed.

Feeling all the pain and depression, she said repeatedly, "I forgive my depression and all the people, including Sheila, who seemed to confirm my lack of self-worth. I forgive all the times I tried to shut out the world." And next, "I forgive myself for choosing depression over love, the love I know exists through my experience of the Inner Spirit." She now took all those awful down feelings and passed them to the Inner Spirit to disappear forever, and immediately she could feel her mood lighten, seeing her future in a new light. Now she was ready to check this off her list.

Hopefully through these examples, you can see some of the experiences and emotions you've had in your life. This process of forgiveness is truly applicable to any negative experience you might have, to any non-loving thought in your mind. As you commit to this practice and continue it for a period of time, forgiveness will become second nature to you. You will know that any non-loving thought which passes through your mind can be freed. You will know you do not have to live with the pain and anger and fear, but can turn it all around through forgiveness.

In the next chapter we will take this to the next level. Up to now we have focused on doing a regular practice, which involves finding some quiet time to get in touch with the Inner Spirit. Now in addition to this regular practice, we will learn how to forgive in real time, clearing away the non-loving thoughts right after they occur. This leads us ultimately to continual forgiveness, and the possibility of finally saying good-by to the ego.

Continual Forgiveness

We began with our philosophy, and using those ideas, you have now learned a simple method to practice forgiveness in your life. If you have followed the steps so far, you should have a list of many non-loving thoughts you have identified in your mind, you should be setting aside time each day to connect with the Inner Spirit, and you should have had some successful attempts at this new way of forgiveness. Hopefully as you have success, you will feel more motivated to continue a regular practice and will devote more time in your life to what you see as an important undertaking.

If you never do anything other than this practice of forgiveness, this practice of releasing your non-loving thoughts, you will in time truly transform your life. As you begin to release these thoughts, you will realize the power they have had over you. These non-loving thoughts have colored every perception you have about the world and about yourself. The ego uses these thoughts to keep you tied to this world.

Once the non-loving thoughts are released, what will open up in their place is the perception of love in the world around you and within yourself. You will begin to feel a new lightness and well-being as you begin to realize you no longer need to live by fear and guilt and anger. There is a way to exist in this world by responding to everything with love. The wonderful thing about this practice is that this will happen inevitably as you continue to show your intent to change.

There is, however, a step beyond this regular practice of forgiveness, a step that will lead you to further transformation and can potentially steer your life in new directions. This step is called continual forgiveness. It's just what it sounds like it is – forgiving the non-loving thoughts in your mind in real time. Whenever you perceive a non-loving thought going through your mind, you will instantaneously forgive and release the thought. In this chapter we will learn how to reach this place of continual forgiveness.

Understanding Continual Forgiveness

Suppose you are walking down the street minding your own business and someone comes out of a store, bumps into you, and then yells at you for getting in his way. Your first reaction might be to yell back, "Hey, Buddy, you ran into me!" The result is an angry exchange. Now suppose you realize in that moment the two non-loving thoughts you had – first the perception of anger directed at you, and then your angry response.

As you continue walking along, you call on the Inner Spirit inside your mind. By practicing forgiveness on a regular basis, you have found it easier all the time to touch this place of peace and love. So now here on a crowded street, you go to this place in your mind and you follow the three steps to forgiveness. You take the non-loving thought of anger, you touch the Inner Spirit, and then you forgive the other party, forgive the illusory event that just transpired, and finally forgive yourself.

This is what continual forgiveness is all about, perceiving a non-loving thought as it occurs, and immediately, or very shortly thereafter, going through the process of forgiveness while going about your normal day. In the beginning, if you are in the middle of a conversation or some other type of concentration, it may be difficult to do this in the moment, but it still can be done a few minutes later when you have a little time to focus on the process. Don't put it off too long, though, because the ego will be at work trying to get you to forget your perception of the non-loving thought, so the emotions of the event can begin to take hold in your mind.

Practicing Forgiveness

Just as we saw in practicing forgiveness, the process becomes easier the more we do it. It becomes easier to identify the non-loving thoughts we have, it becomes easier to touch the Inner Spirit in a non-quiet environment, and it becomes second nature to follow the process of forgiveness. Once you have the first success at real-time forgiveness, you will find yourself on the lookout for non-loving thoughts popping up to be forgiven. You will see how by taking a moment to forgive this thought at once, it has no time to develop power over you. It comes and it goes. That's it.

Once this begins, your life will be moving in a new direction. Previously as you spent time every day practicing forgiveness, you were specifically looking at the thoughts that were in the front of your mind at the time of the practice. During the rest of the day, non-loving thoughts would come and go and these thoughts would influence how you felt throughout the day. Your daily life would be only minimally impacted by your practice.

By starting down the road of continual forgiveness, you now are impacting directly every aspect of your emotional life. Every situation is either a truly loving encounter or an opportunity for forgiveness. If that forgiveness is practiced in real time, then even the angry, fearful, guilt-ridden experiences in your life will in a very brief time be transformed into loving ones. The ego begins to lose control as we listen moment by moment to the Inner Spirit.

In continual forgiveness, you have the promise of a profound change in who you are and how you live your life. The more you practice real-time forgiveness, the freer you will feel, the more loving you will feel, the more peaceful you will feel. You are simply becoming the self you have always been, the self connected to the Mind of God, and this self will know there is nothing that can hurt you or take love and peace away from you without your consent.

There is no more direct path back to God than continual forgiveness. There is no religion, philosophy, procedure, ritual, prayer, or meditation you can do which will change your life more profoundly. There are many paths to remembering our place in the Mind of God, but there is no straighter way to finding our True Home. You have the opportunity through this real-time practice to find what you have been seeking all your life.

Transition to Continual Forgiveness

So if continual forgiveness is such a great thing, why don't we just jump into it from the beginning? There is a reason we presented the practice of forgiveness before talking about continual forgiveness. It is much easier initially to go through the steps of forgiving while being in a quiet place relatively free of distractions than it is to forgive while in the thick of an emotionally upsetting event. You must learn the steps first and apply them over and over to many different types of non-loving thoughts before you will be ready to try continual forgiveness.

What we are trying to avoid is the sense of frustration which comes from not learning a skill adequately before we apply it to critical situations. This is a classic ego ploy – to make you believe you are ready for the big time, knowing you will likely fail and therefore prove to yourself you really aren't worthy. We want to avoid this feeling of failure, so in this section we will present a way to transition into continual forgiveness, and hopefully use the small successes along the way to reinforce the value of this process.

In order to be ready to try continual forgiveness, you should have spent some period of time regularly practicing forgiveness using the list you have created. How long this period of practice should be will obviously vary from person to person. One way to gauge how you are progressing is to observe how many times per week you set aside to practice forgiveness. Another gauge is to notice if you begin to miss the practice when you are away from it for a period of time. You should get to the point where your desire for practicing forgiveness is stronger than your resistance to doing it.

In regard to the frequency of your practice, a good rule of thumb might be that you are able to set aside some time at least four or five days a week, and preferably twice a day. During these sessions you should be addressing two or more items on your list. This means you are forgiving at least fifteen to twenty items on your list every week. Of course, life may interfere at times with travel or personal events which take you away from your schedule. What is important is that these times of interference are not long and you return with a strong intent as soon as possible.

If sitting down for this practice is a chore you feel you are required to do, like writing a term paper in school, then you are not yet ready for continual forgiveness. These moments of true forgiveness should begin to bring you such happiness you won't want to miss a single time. You should get to the point where if something interferes with your practice, you will yearn to be back in communication with your Inner Spirit, spending sacred time forgiving items on your list.

Another reason we don't start with continual forgiveness is that by keeping your list, you are able to collect non-loving thoughts from your past, ones you may not think about too often in the present. Even though the events may have occurred a long time ago, the emotional content may still be strong. By adding items like this to your list and then taking quiet time to deal with them, you can clear away some of these leftover emotions. This makes your regular practice an important complement to continual forgiveness. There may come a day when the practice is no longer necessary, but for now both are important.

Now let's suppose you have a regular practice and you truly look forward to every moment you can spend forgiving with the help of the Inner Spirit. You can now make your first attempts at real-time forgiveness. One way to do this is to write down a suggestion to yourself that you will try to recognize a non-loving thought during the day as it occurs. In the midst of a busy day, you may forget about this suggestion, but if it is made regularly, then some day you will realize you just had a non-loving thought, an angry, fearful, guilty, or sad thought.

Once you've made this realization, try to step away from whatever you are doing and make your connection to the Inner Spirit. Forgive the illusory non-loving thought, focusing on all the details of the experience, forgiving anyone else involved, and finally forgiving yourself. You will have achieved your first real-time forgiveness, and be on the road to continual forgiveness. In the beginning, doing this once or twice a day is plenty. You should still follow your quiet-time practice on a regular basis, so these instances of real-time forgiveness just add to your overall practice.

When you have had some success with forgiving instantaneously, it is really just a matter of doing it more often which will lead you toward continual forgiveness. The only steps required are that you notice a non-loving thought appearing in your mind, you find a moment to focus on the process of forgiveness, and then you go through the same steps you would in your regular practice. Initially the hardest part may be recognizing the non-loving thoughts you have all the time. The ego doesn't want you to observe these thoughts. The ego wants you to get lost in the emotion of the moment and forget about your connection to the Inner Spirit.

If you can begin to see how the ego tries to fool you, if you can see a powerful negative emotional experience as just another non-loving thought, then you will be well on your way to success. Recognition is the key and if recognition becomes the norm in your life, you will find you are forgiving thoughts throughout the day, and once this happens, there will be nothing standing in your way as you realize the wonder and power of continual for-giveness.

Using Continual Forgiveness

In order to make the transition to continual forgiveness, you will need to become more aware of your thoughts. This does not mean you have to be aware right now of every thought in your mind. You probably have hundreds of thoughts in a day and try-ing to capture every one of them would be impractical. What we are looking for at this stage is the more emotionally charged non-loving thoughts. These are the ones which are more likely to be at the front of our awareness, and to which we can more easily apply our process of forgiveness.

One of these thoughts might relate to an immediate event, such as an angry outburst or a painful experience. On the other hand, it might be an emotional thought from long ago which comes back into your mind after being triggered by something in the present. It might be a fear that suddenly arises based on other thoughts or events. The timeframe of the thought is not impor-tant, the emotional content is. It's this emotional content that will allow you to stop your monkey mind thinking for a moment and to focus on the specific non-loving thought.

Once you are able to capture this non-loving thought, you can then take the steps to forgive it in real time. Depending on your situation, you may be able to do it immediately or you may have to wait a few moments before you can follow the steps to for-giveness. It's important not to wait too long, though, because the ego will want you to lose focus so it can get the monkey mind cranking again. Keeping your awareness and focus on the non-loving thought is critical to learning continual forgiveness.

As you make progress in applying real-time forgiveness, you will begin to see how events and thoughts are linked together. It may seem on some occasions that an event will occur that triggers a thought in your mind. It may also happen that you will become aware of a thought, and soon after a related event will occur. There is really no difference. Your thoughts and your experience are fundamentally connected, and starting to learn how to be more aware of your non-loving thoughts will eventually bring you closer to this realization.

So now we'll look at a couple of examples of applying forgiveness in real time. As you'll see, the first step is to catch the non-loving thought in your mind. Then you can go through the steps to forgiveness as soon as you can. The first example will refer to a real-time event and the second will be a triggered memory of a past event.

Example 13:

> Sarah: "The other day I was driving to work and my phone rang and it distracted me for a moment. I veered just a little bit out of my lane and some guy behind me sat on his horn and then yelled obscenities at me as he drove past. I was so pissed."
>
> "The guy that yelled at me on the highway really pissed me off."

Sarah's first reaction to this minor road rage incident is to get angry. It's her way of making the other person guilty. This time, though, right after she feels the anger, she realizes it's happening and she knows this is a non-loving thought ready for forgiveness. So while she's driving, she takes a moment to turn part of her awareness to the place she knows she can find the Inner Spirit. She does her best to maintain a dual awareness, still driving, but aware the Inner Spirit is there.

As she relives the angry exchange in her mind, she says to herself, "I forgive the other driver for his anger, knowing this was a projection of the ego. And I forgive the whole angry experience that just occurred." Then, "I forgive myself for reacting with anger and not with love." As she does this, she takes all the anger from the situation and passes it to the Inner Spirit for release.

What's different this time versus what we did in the last chapter, is the experience has no time to take hold in Sarah's mind. If she had not done this forgiveness in real time, for the rest of the day and maybe for several days, she would have had an uncomfortable feeling leftover from this event. It may have colored other emotional interactions she would have had. By taking on the event immediately and following the steps to forgiveness, the event and all the unpleasant emotions around it are released and eventually forgotten.

Here we see the power of continual forgiveness – strong emotional experiences do not have a chance to take root in your mind. By being aware that a non-loving event has just occurred and then taking the steps to immediately forgive it, Sarah can now be free of the emotions of the event and can proceed to move on with her life. She will no longer be dragged down by these events and feelings, and will be freer to express unconditional love in her life.

Example 14:

> Jason: "I was watching TV the other day and I saw a newborn in intensive care and it brought back everything about Billy's birth. I started feeling really sad."

> "I was feeling sad thinking about Billy's birth."

The shock of discovering Billy's heart problems right after his birth was one of the most emotionally upsetting events in Jason's life. Over the years he has worked on forgiving the experience and the emotions he felt. But this day, he sees another child in a situation similar to what Billy went through, and he lets himself go to the ego place in his mind where sadness and emotional upset are the rule. He actually begins to embrace this sadness, letting it drag him down and even letting it affect other things he's doing.

Then the awareness hits, and he realizes this is another ego-generated non-loving thought. He immediately stops what he's doing and goes to the quiet place in his mind where he sees the form of the Inner Spirit. Almost instantly he begins to lift himself out of his sadness. He holds his dual focus on the sad event and the Inner Spirit, and then says, "I forgive all the sadness around Billy's birth and around the newborn I saw on TV." And, "I forgive myself for choosing sadness over the love I have for Billy and all the others involved." He takes the ugly feelings of sadness and passes them to the Inner Spirit.

As Jason learns to forgive in real time, he can see the non-loving thoughts in his mind more quickly. After having this sadness triggered in him a few times, now he recognizes it instantly and it goes away instantly. This is the promise of continual forgiveness – non-loving thoughts forgiven instantly. Jason continues his regular practice at home, but now he begins to see the promise of real-time forgiveness as well.

As we see in these examples, the key to this process is becoming aware of the non-loving thought as quickly as possible. It's this awareness which leads to the freedom of continual forgiveness. It does require constant vigilance and there will be missteps along the way. No one has to be perfect at this. We just have to do our best to show the intent, the willingness, and the vigilant awareness, and real change will come to our lives.

The Freedom of Continual Forgiveness

In the fourth chapter, we discussed the monkey mind and how the ego uses the cacophony of thoughts, mostly non-loving thoughts, to create the illusion of the world we believe we inhabit. In the world we see in front of us, there is no difficulty finding instances of anger, hate, killing, destruction, fear, and all the other woes we are used to experiencing. There are times of happiness and love as well, but ultimately, if we continue to listen to the ego's chaos of thoughts, we will have trying times in life, knowing death is at the end.

There's a certain stickiness to this world, a feeling the world we are experiencing now is the same world we experienced in the past and the same we will experience in the future. It's the ego that encourages us to feel this and the way it does this is through the stickiness of our non-loving thoughts. By having the same thoughts over and over we maintain the illusion those thoughts project. When we practice continual forgiveness, our non-loving thoughts do not have time to develop stickiness, and therefore, the ego world those thoughts project begins to fall apart. In its place we begin to see a world of love.

We have learned a process here that began with observing the non-loving thoughts in your mind. We learned how to make a list of these thoughts which can be used to practice forgiveness. We then learned the very important step of getting in touch with the Inner Spirit, our connection to God. This led to the three-step process of forgiveness. Once we developed a regular practice, we showed how real-time, continual forgiveness can begin.

It is possible to reach the point where forgiveness is truly continual. As you go about your day, an awareness is triggered every time you have a non-loving thought. You can then take a few moments immediately or soon after to forgive the thought, following the process. As this keeps happening throughout the day, these non-loving thoughts have no time to create a negative pull on you. You are freeing them as soon as they occur.

If you can do this constantly and make it your normal way of acting in the world, you will completely transform your life. If non-loving thoughts have no place in your mind, all that's left is thoughts of unconditional love – kindness, compassion, trust, peace. In one way the world around you may not look any different at all, but because you are different, because your mind is different, your perception of this world will be absolutely changed.

And as you practice continual forgiveness every day, this means you must be constantly touching your Inner Spirit during the day. This will strengthen the bond you feel with your Inner Spirit, and consequently bring you closer to God. You may find you will experience moments of revelation and true communion with God. These moments may be fleeting since living in this world requires we keep some focus here, but the joy and wonder of this communion will be a powerful reminder of the value of your practice.

For your entire life, you have listened to the whisperings of the ego telling you to see a world of separation around you, a world where love is about what you can get out of it, where fear is a reasonable response to the dangers around you, where guilt is inevitable given the imperfect nature of your self. These whisperings have affected every decision you make in life, and every decision you have made out of fear, anger, or guilt will inevitably bring you more fear, anger, and guilt. The ego's thoughts keep this world going.

Now finally you have a tool to frustrate and debilitate the ego. If you take to heart what has been presented to you in this book, if you follow the steps to a regular practice of forgiveness, and if you can begin to experience continual forgiveness in your life, you will at last free yourself from the ego's influence. All that will be left is your experience of the Inner Spirit and ultimately your experience of God.

Where Forgiveness Will Lead

In this final chapter, we will explore a possible future, a future where you have learned this philosophy and this process of forgiveness. It's a future where in addition to regularly practicing forgiveness, you have gone beyond to a true state of continual forgiveness. By learning to forgive in real time, your non-loving thoughts have become fleeting events with no real impact on your life. You are on a new path, choosing the Inner Spirit over the ego. What would this future be like, this future where the ego no longer has power over you, this future where anger, hate, fear, and guilt are meaningless ideas? What would it be like if love, kindness, and compassion were the only emotions you experienced?

How Life Will Change

What would it be like? The first thing to note is that the circumstances of your life may not change much at all. This practice is not about joining a new church or leaving on a quest. It's about a change of mind, and though it will impact how you see and interact with the world, your day-to-day activities might continue as before. You may live and interact with the same people in the same situations, working the same job, observing the same scenery. Nothing in your life *needs* to change, but some things *might* change.

If we were to look from the outside at the lives of Jason and Sarah after they had begun to practice continual forgiveness, we might not notice anything different. Jason would likely still have a family and Billy would still have heart problems. Sarah might still see her sister Sheila, and both Jason and Sarah could be expected to go to work and interact with others during the day.

They most likely would live in the same locations as before and would have no desire to go anywhere else. What would be different would be their behavior, because they would be operating under a simple principle.

'Respond to everything with love.'

With this idea, all of their interactions with others will be transformed. Instead of responding to situations with anger or guilt or fear, they will respond with love. This is the promise of what continual forgiveness can bring to your life. If you can commit to practicing forgiveness, letting the Inner Spirit free you from your non-loving thoughts, and if continual forgiveness can become your usual way of being in the world, the love that is fundamentally who you are can shine through. You can make unconditional love your natural response.

Think back over the last week or two at all the interactions you have had with other people. Think of how many times you have responded to a situation with feelings of anger, guilt, fear, sadness, worry, etc. Now thinking about each of those situations, imagine you had responded instead with love. Go over these interactions one by one and think how this would have altered the experience and the way you would have viewed the experience. You don't know how the other person or persons involved would have reacted, but you would be different because you did not let your non-loving thoughts rule the situation.

This is the beginning of the end for the ego. As long as we are in this world, as long as we seem to inhabit a body, the ego will still be part of who we are. The ego wants us to respond to every situation with anything but love. Now as we go down this road of continual forgiveness, the ego's voice will get quieter and quieter, and the voice of the Inner Spirit, your connection to God, will take its place. You will go from an ego-dominated life with a continuous stream of non-loving thoughts, to a life dominated by love and compassion for all those around you.

Over time your relationships with others may be fundamentally altered. As you express more love in your life, others will perceive this and may respond differently to you. This might lead to new experiences and relationships you had not anticipated before you began this journey. The exact outcome will vary from one individual to the next, but in all cases what really matters is how you feel, the peace and love you feel as you walk through the world, a world you now see in a new light.

From our first look at the philosophy in the second chapter, our goal has been to reach a state of peace. When you are in a state of continual forgiveness, you will be at peace, knowing there is nothing that can ultimately hurt you or rip the peace away from you, for any attempt to alter the peace is just another non-loving thought. You are now living in constant touch with the Inner Spirit, and through this touch, you are aware of your home in the Mind of God. This gives you the power and freedom of living without guilt and without fear, knowing your True Self is eternal and beyond any physical limitation.

Most who reach this stage will continue to live in the physical world for some time, but the experience of that world will be irrevocably changed from the world which existed before. You have made a decision to ignore the will of the ego, and to listen only to the will of the Inner Spirit. This was your choice when you first decided to practice forgiveness in your life. Each time you forgave a non-loving thought, you chose the Inner Spirit again. By making that choice, you accepted the will of the Inner Spirit, knowing you will be safe and loved and at peace. You are on the way Home.

Finding Our New Home

There is another step beyond this state of living at peace in the world. We can only talk about this step with fleeting words and in hushed tones. The world where we lived before we chose separation is a world of oneness, and cannot truly be described in words or images. Using language, we can only suggest what it is like, because this is a world which can only be experienced. As you embrace the Inner Spirit in your life, you will likely touch this other world at times, and when you do, you will know there is something real beyond your everyday life.

This is a place you can call Home. It's not the place you're living now, even with all your family and friends gathered around you. It's not the place you grew up with your parents, grandparents, and extended family. It's not the place you remember where you had really happy times in your life. It's much bigger and more wonderful than any of these places. It's a place where only Love exists, a place beyond the world of the ego. When you find it, you will recognize everything about it and you will wonder how you could ever have forgotten it.

Remember where you came from, the Loving Mind of God. This is all you ultimately have to do, just remember. It isn't necessarily easy, because the ego side of your mind wants to resist every effort you make to recall your True Home. But no matter how much resistance you experience, there is a real inevitability to where you are headed. Once you decide there must be something better in your life, something beyond all the non-loving thoughts which have driven your choices in life, the beauty of this Home will shine as a beacon leading you on in your pursuit of true forgiveness.

The question might arise at this point as to how long this will take. When will I be able to achieve continual forgiveness? And when will I go beyond to find my way Home? Of course, all of this will vary from one person to the next based on understanding, life circumstances, and level of commitment. What's important to realize is it doesn't really matter for two reasons. The first reason is because once you start on the path to forgiveness and begin to appreciate the benefits in your life, time will no longer matter to you. When you are experiencing peace and love, the future will lose its importance and you will live more completely in the present.

The second reason is time has no meaning outside of the ego's world. Your True Self exists within an eternal presence, a place beyond our understanding of time and space. Right now you are There and here at the same 'time'. So to even consider how long it will take to make our way Home is a meaningless question. Time is for worries about a future in this world. Time disappears when we transcend the limitations the ego has worked so hard to maintain within the mind. When we free ourselves of the ego, we will no longer ask questions about time.

Finally you might wonder what it's like to re-experience your Home within the Mind of God. How would it feel? What would that life be like? Millions of words have been written trying to describe spiritual experiences, and no words will ever capture the full experience. Your best hope for getting a glimpse is to regularly connect with the Inner Spirit, the closest one can get to God while still inhabiting the ego world. Make it your commitment to spend time with the Inner Spirit every day, and before long you will no longer have to ask these questions. The Love and Peace of that other world, your Home, will spread through your entire life.

Forgiveness Will Set You Free

You now have all the tools you need. You have a philosophy which includes the concept of a God of Mind, a Loving God, a God that sees guilt in no one. You have seen how the idea of separation has led us to believe we live in this physical world, and how the ego is the part of the mind that tries to maintain the belief in separation. You have discovered how forgiveness can free you from the hold of the ego by seeing your non-loving thoughts as illusions. By getting in touch with the Inner Spirit, our connection to God, you now have the help you need to achieve a state of peace.

You have learned the simple three-step process for forgiveness, a process which can be repeated over and over and applied to all your non-loving thoughts. You have seen multiple examples of how this process can be used with thoughts of anger, fear, guilt, and more. Finally you have learned about continual forgiveness with the realization it's possible to forgive your non-loving thoughts in real time. When you do, the ego begins to recede and what is left is the love and peace which are your birthright. You have the power and the knowledge to change your life to one of love, kindness, and compassion, a life free of the ego.

Now this is my challenge to you. You have a decision to make about your life – 'Do I only want to listen to the ego throughout my life, or do I want to find the Inner Spirit, my connection to God?' If you only choose the ego, then your time spent in this physical world will ultimately be without meaning and purpose. The ego offers you pain, fear, guilt, separation, and eventually death. The ego offers you nothing of lasting value. Only if you can learn to communicate with the Inner Spirit, only if you can learn to express compassion, kindness, and unconditional love in your life, will you find the peace and happiness you seek. Through practicing forgiveness and through remembering your True Self within the Mind of God, you can shake off the shackles of the ego once and for all and return to your True Home.

Make your choice.

Suggested Reading

For further study,

A Course in Miracles, Second Edition, Foundation for Inner Peace, acim.org

Navarro, Edwin, *The End of Guilt: Realizing Your Innocence through A Course in Miracles,* Navarro Publishing, edwinnavarro.com

Wapnick, Kenneth, *The Message of A Course in Miracles, Vol. 1, All Are Called,* Foundation for *A Course in Miracles*, facim.org

Other Books by Edwin Navarro

It's All Mind: The Simplified Philosophy
of *A Course in Miracles*

The End of Guilt: Realizing Your Innocence
through *A Course in Miracles*

Miraculous Ideas: Thoughts on *A Course in Miracles*

Roland's Quest: A Modern-Day Spiritual Journey

Edwin Navarro has been involved in consciousness exploration since the 1970s. After receiving Masters degrees in physics and mathematics, he had a 20-year career as a physicist, software engineer, and entrepreneur. In the late 1990s he left the business world and began a full-time exploration of dreams, meditative states, and the multi-dimensional aspects of consciousness. This led him deeper into the concepts of *A Course in Miracles* and ultimately into writing five books based on the principles of the Course. He lives in Mill Valley, CA.

Contact the author at edwinnavarro.com